FROM HERSCHEL
TO A
HOBNAIL BOOT

FROM HERSCHEL TO A HOBNAIL BOOT

The Life and Times of Larry Munson

Larry Munson
with Tony Barnhart

TRIUMPH
B O O K S

Triumph Books and colophon are registered trademarks of Random House, Inc.

Library of Congress Cataloging-in-Publication Data
Munson, Larry.
 From Herschel to a hobnail boot : the life and times of Larry Munson /
Larry Munson with Tony Barnhart.
     p. cm.
  ISBN-13: 978-1-60078-288-6
  ISBN-10: 1-60078-288-4
1. Munson, Larry. 2. Sportscasters—United States—Biography.
3. University of Georgia—Football—History. 4. Georgia Bulldogs (Football team)—History. I. Barnhart, Tony. II. Title.
  GV742.42.M86A3 2009
  796.092—dc22
  [B]
                                    2009029424

This book is available in quantity at special discounts for your group or organization. For further information, contact:
    Triumph Books
    542 South Dearborn Street
    Suite 750
    Chicago, Illinois 60605
    (312) 939-3330
    Fax (312) 663-3557
    www.triumphbooks.com

    ʾd in USA
        978-1-60078-288-6
        ʿ Patricia Frey
        ʿtion by Sue Knopf

        ʾrʿsy of Larry Munson unless otherwise indicated

Contents

Foreword

Leo Lassen was the sports voice of my childhood.

That's an oblique way to begin a foreword for a book about Larry Munson. Let me try to explain.

Leo Lassen was the radio voice of the Seattle Rainiers baseball team, a Triple A farm club of the Chicago White Sox, during the late 1940s and early '50s. My family lived just north of Seattle from the time I was four years of age until I was 12. I listened to his broadcasts of hundreds of Pacific Coast League games. Now, 50-some years later, I still have vivid recollections of quiet summer nights spent with my ear cocked to the radio as Lassen made the games come alive both through his brilliant descriptive skills and through his fierce loyalty to the team.

Does he remind you of Larry Munson and the Georgia Bulldogs?

Over the decades, I wonder how many hundreds of thousands of young men and women, to say nothing of their parents and grandparents, have listened to Larry's deep, rich voice and his passionate advocacy of his beloved Bulldogs. How many have marveled at his creativity and his unique style and felt that, through him, they were ever more deeply vested in the fortunes of Georgia's teams?

My association with SEC football, through the privilege I've been given of broadcasting games for CBS Sports, only goes back to the turn of the century, to the year 2000. So I had heard *of* Larry Munson long before I actually heard him.

On Saturday evenings in the autumn, our telecast crew will often find ourselves in the midst of fairly lengthy postgame drives, say from Tuscaloosa to Atlanta or from Gainesville to Orlando. Those trips would become a pleasure rather than an ordeal if the Georgia Bulldogs were playing at night and Larry Munson was on the radio.

Fifty years from now, some grandparent is going to remember him as the sports voice of their childhood..

Ultimately, I got to know him personally, and my admiration for him and for his contributions to the craft of broadcasting became great.

"Sugar falling from the sky."

"Run, Lindsay, run!"

"Hobnail boot."

These are all brilliant bits from Larry Munson.

Fifty years from now, some grandparent is going to remember him as the sports voice of their childhood. "Yes," they'll say to a grandson or granddaughter, "[fill in the blank] is good, but you should have heard Larry Munson.

"He was absolutely the best."

—*Verne Lundquist*

Verne Lundquist

Veteran sportscaster Verne Lundquist has been the lead announcer on the CBS SEC Game of the Week *since 2000. Like Larry, Lundquist was born in Minnesota (Duluth). Also like Larry, Verne is a member of the National Sportscasters and Sportswriters Hall of Fame.*
PHOTO COURTESY OF CBS SPORTS

Acknowledgments

I've always believed that in life and in work, when one door closes another one opens. And so it was for me and the opportunity to do this book with Larry Munson.

Last October, after 24 years with the *Atlanta Journal-Constitution,* I was among a group of 73 reporters and editors who took a voluntary buyout to leave the newspaper. Walking away from the *AJC* was one of the toughest decisions I've ever made, but it was the right one.

I knew I would still be very busy for the rest of the 2008 football season with freelance television, radio, and Internet work. What I wasn't sure about was what I was going to do after the season. My answer came when Michael Munson called and asked me to take on this project. It has been a labor of love, and it came at the perfect time in my life.

I want to thank Michael and his wife Susan, who entrusted me with helping Larry tell his incredible story.

I want to thank Claude Felton, Georgia's Hall of Fame sports information director. This is the fourth book where I had to lean on Claude and his staff for a ton of help. He and Karen Huff, his out standing office manager, made all of the research files and information available to me. I couldn't have done it without them.

I want to thank Dan Magill, Georgia's legendary former SID and tennis coach. There is nobody on Earth who knows Georgia or loves Georgia more than Coach Magill. In 1966 he wrote the first release announcing Larry's hiring. He and his friend Billy Joe Brown put together the first audio-highlight tapes of Larry's greatest calls, which allowed the legend of Munson to grow. Coach Magill has always done what is best for Georgia, and I am one of the lucky ones to learn from him, first as a student and then as a professional.

I want to thank Loran Smith, the longtime executive director of the Georgia Bulldog Club, who was the sideline reporter for most of Larry's 43 years as the Voice of the Bulldogs. He is the authority when it comes to the subject of Georgia football and has always been generous with his time and knowledge. Ever since my days as a student at Georgia, Loran has supported me and offered encouragement. I appreciate that.

I want to thank UGA athletics director Damon Evans and associate athletics director Alan Thomas for going beyond the call of duty with their assistance. They understood how much this project meant to Larry and pitched in when we really needed some help.

I want to thank my wife, Maria; my daughter, Sara Catherine; and her husband, Jim. They gave me a lot of encouragement when I left the *AJC* and were thrilled when this project came along. I could not have done it without their support. Maria has been married to a sportswriter for 32 years, which means there is a very special place in Heaven reserved for her.

I want to thank my mother, Sara, who first taught me the love of reading and writing. She, more than anybody, understood what this project meant to me.

And finally I want to thank Larry. He told me that a long time ago he had made up his mind that he was never going to do a book on his life. He said he had once read where actor Sean Connery of James Bond fame said that every book about him had been full of lies. "As soon as I read that, I knew I was never going to do it," Larry told me in our first session.

Lucky for me and lucky for the Bulldog Nation, Larry had a change of heart.

—*Tony Barnhart*

Introduction
To Larry: Thanks
for the Memories

As fate would have it, I was on the road on September 22, 2008, when the word came suddenly with all the force of a hobnail boot to the nose: Larry Munson, the only radio voice Georgia football fans had known for 43 seasons, had just announced that he had called his final game. He was done.

The nice folks at the Macon Touchdown Club allowed me to make my speech early so that I could get back to Atlanta to help work on the story. I threw out 90 percent of the speech I was going to give because everybody there wanted to talk about Larry. And so did I.

I told them my favorite story of the very first time I came face-to-face with the great Munson. It was October 11, 1975, and I was working for *The Red & Black*, the student newspaper at Georgia. Back then the athletic department allowed a representative from *The Red & Black* to travel with the team, and I was chosen to make the trip to Oxford, Mississippi, for the game with Ole Miss.

Because I was a rookie reporter and had absolutely no idea what I was doing, I left for Hemingway Stadium ridiculously early. But when I arrived, there was the lone figure of Larry Munson sitting in the stands waiting for someone to open the press box. I had never met Larry before, and I was nervous about what I would say to the man who was quickly becoming a legend at the University of Georgia.

I had never met Larry before, and I was nervous about what I would say to the man who was quickly becoming a legend at the University of Georgia.

Larry broke the ice and spoke first. He usually does.

"Hey, kid. Do you realize that we're in big trouble over here today?"

He was right, of course. The final score: Ole Miss 28, Georgia 13.

I told the folks in Macon that Larry is as big a part of Georgia football as Vince Dooley, Herschel Walker, and UGAs I–VII. No broadcaster in radio history—and there have been some great ones—has endeared himself more to a fan base than Larry did with Georgia's.

Later on that night as I drove back to Atlanta, the memories really started to hit me. I was 13 years old in 1966 when Larry Munson called his first game as the Voice of the Bulldogs. I fell in love with college football, in large measure, because of Georgia and Larry Munson. I graduated from the University of Georgia, and Bulldogs football—as called by Larry—became a big part of my career.

Then I thought about my daughter. Sara Catherine was born on October 11, 1982, exactly 33 days before Larry screamed, "Look at the sugar falling out of the sky!" at Auburn. Today she has an undergraduate degree and a law degree from the University of Georgia. She is a big-city lawyer now, but she loves her Georgia Bulldogs and, of course, she loves Larry.

Then I realized there were thousands upon thousands of people just like me, who grew up in Georgia, went to Georgia, and made Bulldogs football a very important part of their lives. Georgia football had been a very important part of their parents' lives. Now it was also an important part of their children's lives. There were countless others who never set foot on the Athens campus but who adopted Georgia as their team. They counted on Larry the most to paint the picture of what was happening on those incredible fall Saturdays in Sanford Stadium.

> *I fell in love with college football, in large measure, because of Georgia and Larry Munson.*

And what was the constant across all those generations of Georgia football fans?

Munson.

Players come and go. Coaches come and go. But Munson had always been there. That was about to change.

And as I drove up I-75 in the dark, I knew what all those Georgia fans were feeling on this historic Monday night. For several generations of Georgians, an important milepost in their lives had just been passed.

And God, it was bittersweet.

It is for those people that Larry wanted to write this book.

I mean, where do you start? In the mere confines of a book how do you sum up the life and career of a man who, unbeknownst to him, provided the soundtrack to your life and to the lives of so many others? Like so many of you who are reading this, I knew exactly where I was and what I was doing for some of Munson's greatest calls:

♦ On November 3, 1973, I was driving back to Georgia Southern from my home in Union Point. I had recently decided that I was going to transfer to the journalism school at Georgia in the hope of becoming a sportswriter. I was listening on my car radio when Andy Johnson picked up a loose ball and ran into the end zone for a touchdown to beat Tennessee 35–31. That's when Larry screamed, "My God, Georgia beat Tennessee in Knoxville!"

♦ On November 8, 1975, Georgia made its traditional trip to Jacksonville to play Florida. I had to stay back in Athens but, along with several hundred other students, I watched the game on a big-screen TV at the late, great Fifth Quarter Lounge on the Atlanta Highway. When tight end Richard Appleby took the handoff from Matt Robinson, we collectively held our breath as he threw the ball to Gene Washington for an 80-yard touchdown and a 10–7 victory over the hated Gators. Then the place just exploded. The next week Munson's call that Washington was "thinking of Montreal and the Olympics" and that "the girders were bending" at the old Gator Bowl was played over and over on WRFC Radio in Athens.

♦ In 1978 I was working at the *News & Record* newspaper in Greensboro, North Carolina. Because there was no Internet, the only way I could hear Larry was if the Bulldogs were playing at night. Then I could get in my car and pick up Larry as his voice boomed across the clear channel, 50,000 watts of WSB Radio in Atlanta. I was pounding on my dashboard when Rex Robinson kicked a field goal with only seconds left to beat Kentucky 17–16 and Larry screamed, "Yeah! Yeah! Yeah! Yeah!"

♦ On November 8, 1980, I was in Tallahassee, Florida, on assignment for the *News & Record*. A couple of hours down Interstate 10, No. 2 Georgia was playing Florida. Part of me wanted to drive to Jacksonville, talk my way into the Gator Bowl, and try to get back for my game that night between North Carolina A&T and Florida A&M. Instead, I sat in my little room at the Econo Lodge and watched the game. When Lindsay Scott turned Buck Belue's pass into a 93-yard touchdown, the biggest single play in Georgia football history, I jumped out of my chair with my arms raised and just destroyed a hanging lamp.

After I got through dancing around the room I called my mom back in Union Point. I wanted her to put the phone near the radio so that I could hear Larry scream, "Run, Lindsay!" My mother didn't quite understand why her son wanted to run up his long-distance bill just to hear some guy on the radio. But this is a universal truth that Georgia fans everywhere will confirm: the experience of a big Georgia victory was not complete until you heard what Larry had said about it.

> *I wanted her to put the phone near the radio so that I could hear Larry scream, "Run, Lindsay!"*

The next morning when I checked out of the hotel, I told the manager about his dearly departed lamp. He was a Florida State fan, and when he discovered that I had done the damage while pulling *against* Florida, he didn't make me pay for it.

One of the biggest days of my professional life was September 22, 1984. As a kid growing up in Georgia, my sportswriting heroes were Furman Bisher of the *Atlanta Journal* and Jesse Outlar of the *Atlanta Constitution*. The late Van McKenzie, the sports editor of the *AJC*, had just hired me to be the Georgia beat writer, and on this day the Bulldogs were playing heavily favored Clemson. At kickoff I turned and found Furman Bisher sitting on my left and Jesse Outlar sitting on my right. For a little country boy from Union Point, Georgia, this was really heady stuff.

But the lasting memory of that day was when Kevin Butler walked onto the field to attempt a 60-yard field goal with the score tied at 23–23 with only seconds left.

"Can he actually make this?" Bisher asked me.

"I've seen him do it in practice," I said, hoping Butler wouldn't make me look stupid.

He didn't. I turned up my little radio as loud as it would go and was barely able to hear Larry scream, "Oh my God! Oh my God!" over the roar at Sanford Stadium when Butler's field goal sailed true with plenty of room to spare.

I turned up my little radio as loud as it would go and was barely able to hear Larry scream, "Oh my God! Oh my God!"

Exactly 24 years later to the day, Munson announced that he was through.

There are so many more personal moments like these but, as Larry would say, you get the picture.

Needless to say I was honored when Larry's son Michael called last fall. Larry was finally ready to do a book about his incredible life and wanted me to help him write it. I felt like the coach who just had a national championship football team dropped in his lap. All I had to do was not screw it up.

Starting in December 2008, Larry and I met three times a week, almost always at 1:00 PM. I would come in with my little digital recorder and my list of questions for that day's session. Sometimes we would stay on topic, but other times Larry would veer off and take me on great adventures with his memories of the Big Band Era (which he loved), minor-league baseball (which he also loved), or the old neighborhood in Minneapolis where he grew up. One thing I learned after the first or second session is that you've got to let Larry be Larry. When he jumped off the road of questions and topics that I had so carefully paved for him, he usually took us to a very neat place.

And we laughed. Man, how we laughed.

The finished product is nothing less than Larry's love letter to Georgia football and its fans, to whom he has devoted the past 43 years of his life. But also remember that when he took the Georgia job in 1966 Larry was already 43 years old, and those years included some extraordinary adventures. Larry wanted to share those memories with the Georgia people because they are so precious to him. Even the biggest of Georgia fans will find there is a lot that they don't know about Larry Munson.

Did you know that Larry:

• Has never had a sense of smell? It impacted his service in World War II in a very unusual way.

• Played piano for a week with the acclaimed Tommy Dorsey Orchestra? You might have heard of their lead singer. He was a skinny kid from Hoboken, New Jersey, named Frank Sinatra.

• Was suspended from his radio job in Nashville for some off-color remarks on the air?

• Was a P.A. announcer for wrestling and boxing matches in Minneapolis? He still calls that "the greatest job of my life," next to Georgia, of course.

One thing I learned after the first or second session is that you've got to let Larry be Larry.

• Called a handful of games for soccer's Atlanta Chiefs?

Those are just a few of the new things I learned in my months of hanging out with Larry to do this book.

The best thing about doing this book was giving Larry a chance to tell his story—the whole story, both good and bad—the way that he remembers it. Others may remember some of these events differently. That's fair. They can write their own book.

He talks about the smart decisions and the dumb ones. In 86 years there were a lot of incredible highs and some devastating lows. And he doesn't pull any punches. Some people get skewered pretty good in this book, including Larry himself.

The day after Larry announced his retirement, I wrote a column for the *Atlanta Journal-Constitution* thanking him for many of the

After so many hours of reflection for this book, I think it's fair to say that, more than ever, Larry understands and appreciates the love of the Bulldog Nation that he continues to receive until this day.

memories I have outlined here. I wanted him to know how he had touched my life and the lives of so many others.

After so many hours of reflection for this book, I think it's fair to say that, more than ever, Larry understands and appreciates the love of the Bulldog Nation that he continues to receive until this day. He understands that as long as there are games Between the Hedges and as long as the Redcoat Band plays "Glory, Glory to Old Georgia," he will be forever young. His contribution to Georgia's history is immeasurable.

Larry Munson will always be the Voice, the Heartbeat, and the Spirit of what it means to be a Georgia Bulldog.

And we were all damned lucky to be a part of it.

—Tony Barnhart
Atlanta, GA, 2009

CHAPTER 1

Get the Picture: It's Been a Helluva Ride

After some prodding by my son Michael, I finally tipped my hat to the crowd at Sanford Stadium on November 29, 2008. It was a very emotional day. PHOTO COURTESY OF THE UNIVERSITY OF GEORGIA

Forty-three years? How is that even possible? Hell, I was 43 years old when Joel Eaves hired me at Georgia in 1966. And I'm still here 43 years later getting ready to walk back into that stadium, maybe for the last time? How does that happen?

S aturday, November 29, 2008.

Part of me was looking forward to this day. But the biggest part of me flat-out just didn't want to go. I didn't want to face what I knew I was going to have to face. It wasn't going to be easy. In fact it was going to be pretty damned hard. Pretty damned emotional. I don't handle that stuff well.

After I announced my retirement back in September, I knew this day was coming. I knew that sooner or later I would go back to Sanford Stadium to say good-bye and to say thanks for what the people in that place had done for me for 43 years.

Forty-three years? How is that even possible? Hell, I was 43 years old when Joel Eaves hired me at Georgia in 1966. And I'm still here 43 years later getting ready to walk back into that stadium, maybe for the last time? How does that happen?

I really didn't think about the fact that we were playing Georgia Tech or the meaning of the game. Georgia Tech is always a big game for us, and early in the week I was really worried about our defense. We just didn't have that stud defensive end like David Pollack that we usually have. We just didn't seem to have the athletes to slow down Georgia Tech, who had been running the ball up and down the field on everybody. And how did they get so good all of a sudden?

But by the time we got to Saturday, I wasn't thinking about any of that. I was thinking about myself and what this day was going to mean. This made it official. I was going away, and that was kind of bothering me. Because to tell you the truth, right up until this time there was still a part of me that thought I could come back. I had been through a tough deal with brain surgery and rehab, but I thought it was just a matter of time before everything was right again.

This made it official. I was going away, and that was kind of bothering me.

3

I had problems with my back, my brain, and just about every body part you can name. I thought that no matter what, the voice would always be there. But it wasn't. I really thought I would be able to work a little longer, but you forget how old you are. And damn it, I was old.

Regardless of everything that had happened to me over the years, I never, ever thought my voice would fade off.

So here you are. My sons Michael and Jonathan and their families are in the house getting ready to go do this thing. I'm not saying a whole helluva lot. I was probably pretty tough to get along with that day.

• • •

This whole deal really started the year before, when I finally decided that the traveling was just killing me. Damon Evans (the athletic director at Georgia), Claude Felton (Georgia's longtime sports information director), and Loran Smith came out to the house to talk about what we were going to do with the radio broadcast in 2007.

Before that meeting I had pretty much made up my mind that I was just going to do the home games that season. I found out later that was kind of what Damon had on his mind and that Claude was ready to support him on the idea. So when Damon brought it up, I immediately said "Yeah." I thought it was a good idea for Scott Howard to do the road stuff. We got through the whole thing in about 45 seconds. The idea of not having to scramble to and from the Atlanta Airport really appealed to me. I could see the look of relief on their faces, because I'm sure they were worried that I might fight it.

It didn't dawn on me that my voice might be so bad that there was no choice whatsoever in this—that I had lost something in my pipes without realizing it. Until you actually open your mouth to call a game, you really don't know. But at the time there was no doubt in my mind that this was the right thing to do. My thinking was that it wouldn't be too offensive to people if Scott and I just split the games. I know you sort of have to sell the idea to sponsors and stuff.

To me it was okay. It didn't bother me at all. Frankly I was a little surprised at my own thinking, because 10 years ago it would have bothered me a lot. But Georgia football is such a big thing, and our audience is really in tune and intelligent about the sport. I knew they would understand.

The thing that kills you when you get older is getting on and off of planes, getting to the airport, getting up to all these different press boxes. I was having back problems, and some arthritis was starting to kick in. The travel just totally exhausts you, and then you have nothing left to do the game. I remember (longtime Kentucky radio voice) Cawood Ledford telling me near the end for him that it was getting tougher and tougher for him to see. He told me, "Munce, I can't get up the first step of the bus."

So I decided just to do the home games. To me, that was the best thing to keep me going for as long as possible.

So in 2007 I did the home games and then went over to Atlanta for the Georgia Tech game at the end of the year. We had a pretty good season (10–2) and got invited to play in the Sugar Bowl against Hawaii. My plan was to make the trip to New Orleans and do the game.

So I decided just to do the home games. To me, that was the best thing to keep me going for as long as possible.

I don't remember all of the details of why I didn't make the trip to New Orleans. It made sense to do the game. There was some publicity with it because the other guy (Hawaii) thought he was good enough to hang with us. Fans wanted to see the game to see what we were going to do with that scoring machine. I don't know why I backed away, but all of a sudden I didn't want to touch it. In the background waiting for you is always the plane that you have to catch the next morning. I just decided not to go.

I didn't know what the problem was, but I was starting to have some spells where I would suddenly black out and fall. I can remember a couple of nights when I would find myself on the ground or halfway on the ground. I know it shocked some of the people around me. I wasn't completely aware of what was happening, but it knocks you for a loop and scares the hell out of you. I would wake up and I would be on the ground. I didn't know what the hell was going on, and I didn't remember a thing. It would just happen

The doctor told me I had a blood clot on the brain and that it was going to have to come out. I was told by the brain-surgery people that I could not take another blow to the head in this place. I hate doctors and I hate hospitals, but it was something we had to do. (Note: On April 4, 2008, Larry had surgery to remove a subdural hematoma from his brain. The surgery was performed at St. Mary's Hospital in Athens, Georgia).

> *The doctor told me I had a blood clot on the brain and that it was going to have to come out.*

I had to go to Atlanta to do some rehab work at the Shepherd Center. I called it the Tech place because all of those Georgia Tech people were hanging around there. I don't think a lot of people knew about that at the time. I didn't know if I wanted to go to Shepherd, but Mixon Robinson, who played for us and went on to become a great doctor, convinced me that this was the way to go. I trusted him.

When you get to Shepherd they are scared to death that you are going to fall and hit your head again in a serious way. And they don't want that. So they strap you into your bed because they don't want you getting up in the middle of the night and going to the bathroom. That was kind of a tough fight. I didn't like that very much.

God, they train you like Rocky over there. They work the hell out of you. At least that was the way it seemed to me. They make you do all of the little dumb things that you never would have thought of doing yourself.

I was there about a month and finally came home sometime in May and started doing more rehab back at Athens Regional Hospital. I had to do the physical therapy, but I also had to do some speech therapy to try and get my voice back to the way it used to be. The speech therapist told me she had been listening to me since she was a little kid. So at least she knew what I was *supposed* to sound like.

After I got back from Shepherd I was feeling a lot better. I knew I had some work to do, but at that point there was no doubt in my mind that I was going to work the home games for the 2008 season. I needed some help getting ready, and I got it from a lot of friends, including Louis Phillips, my longtime spotter. Louis and I would go to Athens Regional Hospital. He would bring the spotting boards that we would use during the games and a tape for that particular game. We would steel ourselves and pretend we were doing the games in the stadium. We would watch the game, I would call the action, and Louis would do the spotting on the boards. A therapist sat there and watched everything that we were doing.

What they were trying to determine was whether or not I could actually do play-by-play again. As we went through it I began to feel pretty confident that I could come back. We did about four or five of those sessions, and when they were over, we didn't anticipate any problems whatsoever. I felt *What they were trying to determine was whether or not I could actually do play-by-play again.* good about what I was doing. That's why later on it would be such a disappointment when I realized I was still a step or so behind.

Later in the summer, after practice started, we went to the stadium to watch Georgia scrimmage. The therapist was convinced that the only way we were going to know for sure if I was ready was to get outside and do something that was pretty close to a real game. It was different than doing the games on television, and it probably wasn't as smooth as I would have liked it to be. There were a bunch of people who were sitting behind us who wanted to watch and listen. But I still thought I was going to be okay. Whatever problems I had, I figured I could talk right through them.

But after that scrimmage, part of me knew damn well that it wasn't going to work. I just didn't want to admit it to myself.

I did the first game against Georgia Southern. I was looking forward to it. I felt there would be interest in the crowd about me, and my interest was up because Georgia Southern is a state rival, and there was an option problem there that we would have to deal with. Once the game started I thought that my voice was high. And when I would go reaching for something with the voice it simply wasn't there. You keep clearing your throat, thinking that your voice is going to come back. But it wasn't coming back, and after the Georgia Southern game I knew it.

And when I would go reaching for something with the voice it simply wasn't there.

The next week I did the Central Michigan game hoping that the next time out it would be better. Maybe I was just rusty the week before and the voice just needed to get back in shape. But the voice, which had never let me down, was going up and dying off. It wasn't going to happen. I knew my voice wasn't where it should be.

When you go through all that rehab and stuff, you don't think for one minute that you can't come back. The one thing that I had always been able to rely on was my voice. But the more and more I tried to use it, the thinner and thinner my voice became. I thought I might have problems in a big game in a big atmosphere, but I was even struggling in these first two games. It's a really strange thing, boy, and at that point you've got to know that you absolutely need to step out...to just go away.

The one thing that I had always been able to rely on was my voice.

Charlie Whittemore drove me back to the house after that second game (with Central Michigan). I can remember that I just wanted to get into the house and turn on whatever big game was on television. I just wanted to see a big, important game.

My mind was racing. I just wish I could remember all those thoughts that were in my mind at the time. But I knew something was wrong, and I remember feeling that I was probably done. I guess I must have felt that I really stunk up the joint.

Michael seemed to be satisfied when I told him I could not go on. I had said to him before that this was coming, but at that point he was ready to argue. This time he accepted it pretty quick. There must have been some moments he heard when I was not doing it right.

There were people we had to talk to, and Michael helped me make those calls. I had to talk to Marc Morgan (the chief operating officer of WSB Radio). He and Damon Evans had made it clear to me that it was my call. They felt that after all this time I should be able to go out on my own terms.

There was never really any real worry on my part about the broadcast because Scott Howard was there. He had been patiently waiting. I had told him to be patient because it was coming for him. It would all be coming. So Scott, who is a solid guy and has a great family, just waited. That helped me a lot. We could have had some guy who was full of flea powder and was ready to blow up the world and start World War Seven! That would have been very tough.

They let me tread water the next week (Georgia had a road game at Arizona State the next Saturday, September 20) and make up my mind. It was difficult. It is damned difficult to admit that you're done.

(Note: On Monday, September 22, 2008, the University of Georgia announced that Larry Munson, who had been the Bulldogs' radio voice since 1966, was retiring effective immediately. Scott Howard would take over play-by-play duties for the rest of the season, beginning with Saturday's home game with Alabama).

When the announcement was made that I was retiring, the whole damn world was calling. I have a caregiver who stays with me, and I just told her that I didn't want to talk to anybody. I went to bed early. What are you going to say? The time had come. When I was done I knew I was done.

When the announcement was made that I was retiring, the whole damn world was calling.

I had always had a plan for the days when I was done calling the games for Georgia. When the first game came around after I quit, I was going to be out in the boat fishing and listening on the radio. That is how I would get away and deal with it. But the first game against Alabama was at night, so I didn't get to do that. I was at home with Michael when the Alabama game came on that night. I went to bed early.

• • •

On the morning of the Georgia Tech game, Charlie Whittemore showed up early like he always did. A lot of folks don't know this, but Charlie made it possible for me to work a lot longer than I thought I would be able to. He was one of our great wide receivers, and then he became a coach under Vince Dooley. Then he got into administration at Georgia, where he was in charge of travel and a lot of different things. I can't tell you how many great things Charlie did for those of us who were traveling with the team.

Several years ago just getting to the press box in Athens—fighting the traffic, getting parked, all of that stuff—was just killing me.

So Charlie basically took me on as his project. On game days he would come to my house and take me and any of my family to the game. And when the game was over, he would get us back home. Traffic in Athens on game day has always been a bad thing, but when you get older it gets worse. And when I started having a tough time getting around because of my back, what Charlie was doing for me meant everything. He really went beyond the call of duty.

There were a lot of people doing stuff behind the scenes that really prolonged my career. Michael Kahn, a big Georgia supporter out of Charlotte, allowed me to fly home from road games on his private jet. That kind of stuff really adds up and helps with the wear and tear on your body.

So we all piled into Charlie's truck and headed to the stadium. And let me tell you, Charlie knows every back street in Athens. I was always amazed at how he could get us through that traffic, and suddenly we were at the stadium. I don't remember a lot about how we got there, but every now and then he would roll down the windows to show the cops who he was carrying around, and the cops would kind of let us through. That was a great deal.

I don't remember a lot about how we got there, but every now and then he would roll down the windows to show the cops who he was carrying around, and the cops would kind of let us through.

We got to the stadium and kind of slipped in the press box because we didn't want anybody to see us and make a fuss. Right about then I was getting pretty quiet because I didn't know what was going to happen. All I remember is that we stayed in one of those extra press boxes for most of the first quarter. The ceremony was going to take place between the first and second quarters.

When the time came to go down to the field, we walked down to an elevator. That's when a bunch of the fans saw me and started saying stuff. I don't remember what all they said, but I remember thinking at the time that the people were very nice.

We got off the elevator, and they put me and my granddaughter, Madeline, into a golf cart. At some point UGA, our mascot, got in the cart with us.

Then suddenly we were through the gate at one end zone and out onto the field. And there was this big roar. It was a cold, rainy kind of day, and here were all these photographers and media guys just going nuts. I didn't expect that. But I really didn't know what to expect.

The crowd suddenly got louder. I was standing there with Damon, not quite sure what I should do. There was a tribute playing on the video board. I had never been in a situation like that before. All of a sudden you find that you can't control your emotions. It's hard to keep a straight face because you can't keep the tears out of your eyes. You kind of want to choke or sob a little bit. Michael told me that he and Whittemore were off to one side because they were having trouble. I even heard that some of my old crew up in the radio booth were having a tough time with this thing.

All of a sudden you find that you can't control your emotions. It's hard to keep a straight face because you can't keep the tears out of your eyes.

It was an emotional moment because the thing you try not to say to yourself is, "I'm done. I'm through. I can never do this again." That kind of stuff can bother you, because at that moment I was thinking that my whole career from Wyoming to Vanderbilt to whatever…was now gone. It had all ended, and that was a little hard.

All of those days way back in Cheyenne when I replaced Curt Gowdy…all of those nights of high school football…all of those Saturdays doing college football…

I was trying really hard not to put a final grade on this thing. I tried not to do that.

I guess I was just sort of standing there kind of in a trance, not sure what I was supposed to do.

Finally it was Michael who broke it, when he barked at me, "Dad, you've got to wave to the people!"

That's when I took off my cap and started pointing to each section of the crowd. And every time I would point at a new section, it would get a little louder. The students really made that moment special. They have always been great to me.

Damon presented me with a painting by Atlanta artist Steve Penley. Then it was time to get back into the cart and go. In a lot of ways it didn't seem real. I figured I had taken more time out there than I was

The students really made that moment special. They have always been great to me.

supposed to. I remember that the crowd continued to be very loud. Someone told me later that they were yelling, "Larry! Larry!" as we headed off the field.

We went back to the press box, but at halftime I was ready to go. People were asking me if I wanted to do this or wanted to do that. But mostly I just wanted to get out of there. I just didn't feel like sitting through the second half of the game. The whole thing had been pretty draining. I wanted to go home and see what else was going on during the games that day.

Once I got home I finally had a chance to think about the 43 years at Georgia and how quickly they had gone by. I had a chance to think about all of the great players and coaches and people I had met. I thought about how damned lucky I was to do something I really loved for so long. I spent what, 60-something years working in the Southeastern Conference? That's a long time, and it was a lucky time for me.

I never thought I was going to work 100 years. A lot of guys don't get to do that.

Could I have made some smarter decisions? Sure. I've made mistakes. A lot of them. I had a couple of marriages that did not work. I could have done a lot of things differently. But there was a lot more good than bad. I've had a lot of great things come my way. There were a lot of bitter disappointments. But when that day was over, I decided that it had been one helluva ride.

And it all started in Minnesota.

> *Could I have made some smarter decisions? Sure. I've made mistakes. A lot of them.*

CHAPTER 2
Memories of Minnesota

With my dad, Harry, at Lake Augusta in 1946. We had our very best talks at the lake. I wore that porkpie hat all the time.

*So he went out and bought me
a brand-new tackle box
just like his. Then he put half of
the stuff from his tackle box
into mine. He told me that
while I was gone he was going to
build up my tackle box because
"you'll be back." Of course,
I didn't think I would ever
be back. I was going on a
great adventure.*

When you get to be my age you remember things in bits and pieces. Memories come to you about a fishing trip, or a football game, or a movie, or an afternoon spent with your family, or that good-looking girl you were trying so damn hard to impress.

That's the way it is with me and Minnesota. Things come to me out of nowhere—little things that at the time seemed to be very, very big things. It's been a long time since I left, but a lot of who I am goes back to my days as a boy in Minneapolis.

It was a great place to grow up if you liked hunting and fishing, and thanks to my dad, Harry, I loved both.

My dad loved sports, but he didn't get a chance to play very long. He was the center on the South High football team in Minneapolis when he quit school and went to work with his dad in the brickyard. That took him right out of the sports thing. That really surprised me. But there are so many things that we did together that made me love sports.

I'm not sure why, but my dad loved speed skating. Minneapolis was the home of Ken Bartholomew and a bunch of skaters who competed in the Olympics (Note: Ken Bartholomew won the silver medal in the 500-meter speed skate in the 1948 Olympics). He would shield me from the wind and hold me so that it looked like the skaters were coming right at me. The skates would make so much noise.

My dad would take me to watch those guys skate, and he would find a spot right on the turn.

They had semipro football at the old Minneapolis Triple A ballpark. They would play a doubleheader, one game at 1:00 and the other at 3:00. I can still remember my dad tucking me into the box seat with a blanket so that I wouldn't get cold. He could've given you the name of every guy on every team. The players had been stars in high school, and we grew up wanting to be those guys. One day we took one of my uncles from Sweden to the game. The first time the team got in a huddle it just bewildered him. He couldn't speak a word of English, but he said something like, "By golly, I would like to hear what they are saying." He was serious about it.

My dad was an insurance salesman. He would leave home every Monday and wouldn't come home until late Friday afternoon. He would tour the state selling and collecting premiums for property and casualty insurance. Whenever he came home on Friday we could hear him whistling as he came into the house, and my sister Dorothy and I would jump up to greet him. He would always have a present for us. But then on Monday he would be gone again, and I really missed him.

I really looked up to him because he taught me so much. I will never forget that first day that we went out in the boat together. We got into a school of walleye pike, which was the king fish of our lake. As soon he got a couple in the boat, he turned them over to show me the difference between the male and the female. He was trying to pick that opportunity to teach me something. He wanted to make damn sure I knew that.

We would sit out in the fields waiting on the pheasants, and he would just talk to me.

He took me on hunting trips. We would sit out in the fields waiting on the pheasants, and he would just talk to me. Sometimes we would go hunting in the snow, and we would use Mom's sheets for camouflage. We would cut out holes for the eyes and nose. We would just ruin the sheets, and mom would really love that.

But dad could make me mad, too. One of my jobs was to cut the grass, and I had to cut it every week while he was gone. It was a small yard, so it wasn't a big job. But dad wanted the grass cut a certain way and in a certain direction. I can't tell you how many times he came

18

home, put on his old clothes, and went out and cut the grass in a completely different direction. Man, that frosted me!

He would come to the back of our house when I was outside practicing my dropkick. We had two poles holding up the clothesline, and they made the perfect goal post. I would kick it between them, and the ball would hit the back of the house. He was afraid that I was going to break a window, but he didn't make me stop. We couldn't play in the street, because if the police caught us they would take our ball away. We were always looking out for the police because we knew they were going to take our damn ball. That happened a couple of times, but every time it did my dad would come home on Friday with a new ball for me.

We were always looking out for the police because we knew they were going to take our damn ball.

I remember when I bought my first shotgun, strictly against orders, while dad was out of town. It was a 16-gauge single shot. I think it cost about $13, and I took the street-car to downtown Minneapolis to buy it. When I got back some nosy neighbor saw me walking down the street with the gun. "Bud Munson [my nickname back then was Bud], you're really going to get it from your mom and dad when they see that gun," she said. The woman was right about my mom, Esther. She was scared of that gun. When my dad got home she told him to take me down to the basement and wear me out. He took me down to the basement, but he didn't wear me out. He just said, "Why didn't you tell me you wanted to do this? I could have gotten you something a lot better from the game wardens I know." It's amazing how such little things still stick in my mind.

I remember when I suddenly told him one day that I was leaving to go replace Curt Gowdy in Cheyenne, Wyoming. I was just think-ing about the excitement of the job and nothing else. He was thinking about the fact that he was about to lose his fishing buddy. Of course,

I was too young and stupid to think about how he was feeling. He had just bought himself a brand-new tackle box at Warner Brothers Sporting Goods on East Lake Street in Minneapolis. And I know he wanted to keep my mind where he wanted it. So he went out and bought me a brand-new tackle box just like his. Then he put half of the stuff from his tackle box into mine. He told me that while I was gone he was going to build up my tackle box because "you'll be back." Of course, I didn't think I would ever be back. I was going on a great adventure.

He died young and suddenly. He was in his sixties. I didn't realize how hard that was going to hit me. All of these thoughts go through your mind. You think about all the things you did, but you also think about the things you didn't do and the things you should have done. I got the call from my sister, and I had to be back in Minneapolis by the next day. I remember sitting there in this little cubbyhole in the church where they put the family of the deceased, and all of these people would come by and pay their respects at the casket. I couldn't believe how many people turned out and said how important my dad was to them. I remember looking into the casket and noticing that his glasses weren't on. My mother thought he should have had his glasses on.

I couldn't believe how many people turned out and said how important my dad was to them.

It was hard to have him gone. But at that point in my life, when I was trying to make it, I was in a hurry all the time. Going somewhere and making a speech for $150 was really a big thing then. I was afraid to slow down.

I don't remember when it was, but one day a package came for me from Dorothy. She had been cleaning out the old house in Minneapolis and found the tackle box that my dad had bought for me. I just put my arms around it. I don't remember if I cried or not, but I remember that I did feel that I was reconnecting with him. So many great memories came back.

I still love to fish because he taught me to love it. But I can't go fishing and not think of him. Sometimes when I'm out there by myself I talk to him. I still miss him a lot.

• • •

As a family we used to go to a movie every Saturday night. My sister and I would argue about what kind of movie we were going to see. She wanted love; I wanted adventure.

I had a very unusual relationship with my sister. We fought like brothers and sisters do. She scoffed at everything I did, and I scoffed at everything that she did. But the fact is that I never really thought of her as a human being until she got married and moved away. She met this guy, fell in love, and then she moved out to California with him and started having babies. Then her husband got caught with another girl, and it looked like the marriage was going to fail.

I remember coming home late one night, and my parents were both awake. They had just gotten a letter from Dot about what was going on in the marriage. I remember my dad saying, "Bud, you've got to pray." So I did, because I was afraid not to.

She came home for a visit and asked me to take her to the show like we used to when we were kids. And during the show I just kept glancing at her with her knees drawn up in the chair. She was so brokenhearted. She seemed so human. That made a big impression on me.

When the police weren't around, we would play ball in the street. Our neighborhood had about 15 boys and 10 girls almost all the same age. We would play softball in the summertime, the boys against the girls. The trees were our bases. Suppertime would come, and that would break up the game. But in the summer when the weather was warm we could get another game going after supper. In the fall we would get the girls to put on jeans and sweaters so we could play tackle football. *We* knew what we were doing. *They* knew what we were doing. But we didn't know that they knew what we were doing. All we wanted to do was tackle them and get our arms around them.

In the fall we would get the girls to put on jeans and sweaters so we could play tackle football.

My mom would sew numbers on a jersey for me for the neighborhood football games. My number was 6. And I can still remember playing on Saturdays, and we would stop and look up into the sky. There was a smoke writer up there, and he would write the halftime score of the Minnesota game in the sky. And if Minnesota was winning, that would just be the greatest thing.

I had a bunch of jobs growing up. One of them was as a lifeguard at Lake Hiawatha. I worked for the Park Board. I only saved two kids. I thought that was pretty good until Ronald Reagan became president, and they said he saved 72. I don't know how in the hell one guy could save 72 people in one summer. I heard it was because he was on the Illinois River and people would come by him on rafts that would go by a mile a minute. He would throw them a rope and pull them back in. I had a lot of respect for Reagan.

The two I saved were like 10 and 13. The 10-year-old was a little problem, because he went down quickly. I was in a wooden rowboat, and I remember dragging my shins across the side of that boat and ripping a bunch of skin off. When I got my hands on him he locked onto me pretty good. It was nothing great, but I got him out.

The 13-year-old was a little more difficult, and later on it made the front page of the Minneapolis paper. I remember going down to the grocery store to pick up some things for my mom, and all of these people started congratulating me. I didn't think much about it then.

If it happened today I'd be cutting out all the pictures and stories and saving them.

One of the first jobs I ever had using my voice was at the old Minneapolis Auditorium downtown. I was the P.A. announcer for the wrestling and boxing matches. The place seated about 12,000, and man, when you climbed into that ring it was really something.

The first night I was in that ring Bronko Nagurski was in one corner and a guy who used to play tackle at Southern Cal was in the other corner, and they were wrestling. It was a helluva thrill because Nagurski was so big. He was an All-American at Minnesota in two different positions—defensive tackle and fullback—and just an enormous man.

The first night I was in that ring Bronko Nagurski was in one corner and a guy who used to play tackle at Southern Cal was in the other corner, and they were wrestling.

I can still remember him taking off his robe in the ring and laying it over the top strand of the rope. He grabbed the ropes and started pulling on them to loosen up, and he was looking at me waiting for me to do something. God, he was huge!

I can remember seeing so many great boxing matches in that place. Guys like Willie Pep and Sandy Saddler who were these tremendous featherweights. I never forgot that job. I've had a lot of thrills in my life, but there was nothing like watching Bronko Nagurski take off the robe. He later opened up a gas station in his hometown of International Falls, Minnesota. It was the last station before you went into Canada. That's all he ever wanted to do. Man, that was the best.

Minneapolis was just a great place to grow up. I really loved the city. We had simple pleasures because life was just so simple. Kissing a girl in a garage? How could that mean so much? But at that moment it meant everything.

CHAPTER 3

My Mom,
My Music

When Frank Sinatra died, every musician who ever played with him got
this photo with a gold record. This one still hangs in my kitchen. I played
with Sinatra and the Tommy Dorsey Orchestra for one unforgettable week
when I was still in high school.

My sister gave me hell because she knew I could have been pretty good if I had worked at it and done it right. I got a couple of shots with some really good bands, and it would have been for pretty good money.

My mother, Esther, grew up just north of Minneapolis. She had three sisters, and they all turned out to be wonderful musicians. They all took piano lessons, and one of them was good enough to have her own radio show across the river in St. Paul.

My mother was very, very good on the piano. Of course she taught me and my sister how to play. Dorothy became a wonderfully trained classical piano player because she worked hard and did what Mother told her to do. My sister was brilliant on the piano.

I wasn't. I was lazy, and I didn't want to put in the work. I just wanted to play by ear because that was fun. When I was practicing, my mom would come up behind me, and all of a sudden there would be a hand on my shoulder. She knew the chords were wrong and that I was just trying to fake my way through it.

But I still learned a lot about music from watching her. She wound up singing with a big women's choir, and she became a soloist. They weren't singing classical stuff, but it was close to it. I went a few times with my buddy Dick Klein, and we sort of giggled our way through it. Man, that would make her mad.

I wasn't great, like my sister, but I could play well enough to think I might be able to do something with my music. Then one day the phone rang. The Tommy Dorsey Orchestra was in Minneapolis for a week, and their piano player, Milt Raskin, had come down with a case of appendicitis. They were looking for a local guy who could fill in for the week.

There was another piano player at Roosevelt High School. His name was Joey Hessberg, and God he was good. He could read music and would have been perfect for the job. But for some reason Joey was out of town that week, and so they offered the job to me.

I was cheating on the chords, and I couldn't fool her. I couldn't fool her about anything.

I remember that my mom bought me a new dark suit with a dark tie and a nice white shirt. She drove me down to the RKO Orpheum Theater, where Dorsey's band was playing. She wouldn't go into the theater with me, so I had to find my way back to the stage by myself. I found the piano and just sat there. Finally the music showed up.

You have to understand how nervous I was, because everybody in the band was famous. Buddy Rich was the drummer, and when he would hit a rim shot, the band came out roaring, and chills went up and down my spine. Ziggy Elman was the lead trumpet, and man, could he play! The first song was called "Well, Git It," which was a big hit by Dorsey's band. I was just out there holding on for dear life and trying to keep up with all of those pros.

> *Buddy Rich was the drummer, and when he would hit a rim shot, the band came out roaring, and chills went up and down my spine.*

The place was packed that night, over 3,000, because of the skinny lead singer. Frank Sinatra was about 26, eight years older than me. And the women just went nuts over that guy. When he started singing they were just screaming. The kids in the crowd had seen what had happened in New York and all of the other big cities where Sinatra had sang. They wanted to copy that, so they were in the aisles dancing and doing all kinds of stuff. He had just cut a song called "This Love of Mine," and it was really sweeping the country. He had not made a movie yet, so his career hadn't really taken off. What I remember about Sinatra is that he really liked the lead singer of the Pied Pipers, Jo Stafford.

For a kid like me, who didn't know what the hell he was doing, it was quite an experience. You know what happened to Sinatra. He went on to become as big as you can be. One day, not too long after he died (on May 14, 1998), I got a package in the mail. It was a photo of Sinatra along with one of his gold records, "My Kind of

Town." The musicians union had sent it out to everybody who had ever played in a band backing up Sinatra. It still hangs in my kitchen.

When you get an opportunity like that and get a taste of what that life is like, you start thinking that you might want to do it for a living. I loved music and thought it would be the greatest thing in the world to travel around from city to city and just play. Whenever I would hear Glenn Miller or Benny Goodman, I would just stop and listen because I was so wrapped up in music. It was so much fun sitting down with guys who were older than me and better than me and learning from them. And some of the girls who sang were really

I loved music and thought it would be the greatest thing in the world to travel around from city to city and just play.

attractive too. I thought that was what I wanted to do with my life. That's why my mom stayed on me so hard. She knew I wasn't going to make it if I didn't do it the right way.

My sister gave me hell because she knew I could have been pretty good if I had worked at it and done it right. I got a couple of shots with some really good bands, and it would have been for pretty good money. "Bud, you can't do that," she said. "You're not ready for that." Of course I would do it anyway and try to fake my way through it.

I would listen to records of the great black bands and try to play what they were playing. I could fool some people, but I couldn't fool my sister.

Right after I graduated from high school I got some offers to tour with some pretty good bands and saw what life on the road was like. The first girl I ever rode with on the band bus was Eugenie Baird. She was a vocalist for the Glen Gray Band, and I fell hopelessly in love. I think she was using me as a bodyguard to keep the other musicians off of her. I sat next to her all the way from Omaha, Nebraska, to

Madison, Wisconsin. She was so good-looking, even when she put her hair up in curlers. And I was so young she probably wanted to make sure that nobody kidnapped me. It was great.

Years later Jeff Van Note and I were doing some talk radio in Atlanta, and I started talking about Eugenie Baird. We were on WSB, which is a clear channel you can hear all over the country at night. A guy called in from Indianapolis and said he knew Eugenie Baird because she lived just right down the street from him. How incredible is that?

God, I was so young and stupid and in love with the idea of being in love. (Note: Eugenie Baird died on June 12, 1988.)

The thing I remember most about touring with the bands is that I felt alone, always alone. But I don't think I ever resented it. I just thought it was part of the great adventure. When you're that age you always think that what you're doing is part of a movie or something. I remember that when the band would take a break I would stay up there on the stage and do a little Basie stuff. A crowd would gather around me. It made me feel good and special. I really loved it.

God, I was so young and stupid and in love with the idea of being in love.

Those were great times, and there was great music. I met some guys who could really blow. But I knew if I was going to make a career out of music, I was going to have to do a lot of work. It was going to take years of studying, because I never really learned how to read music like my mom had tried to teach me. And I had played enough of the good clubs to know that you really had to know how to cut it to stay up with these guys. You never knew when somebody like Count Basie was going to be sitting in the back of the room scouting for new talent. You were getting new music all the time, and you had to be able to read it and be ready to play.

But I stuck with it and continued playing when I went into the service. I ended up at McCloskey General Hospital in Temple, Texas. I started putting together a band that was the nucleus of the old Jimmie Lunceford Band. Then all of a sudden they called me and were going to ship me home. If I had been smart I would have found a way to stay in the service, because that was going to be a helluva band.

When I got home from the service there was a shortage of musicians all over the country. So many bands were losing their guys to the draft, so my phone was ringing all the time. I got a lot of work and had chances to tour with a bunch of bands. My mother didn't like that.

So many bands were losing their guys to the draft, so my phone was ringing all the time.

I was ready to hit the road with a great 10-piece band. My mother and I had a big discussion in the kitchen, and I lost. As it turned out, that entire band was almost wiped out in a truck accident somewhere between St. Paul and Stillwater, Minnesota. My mother was convinced that this was a gift from the Great Father. She held that over my head forever.

When the radio sports thing came around I knew it was time to put that part of my life behind me. But I did learn this: once the music walks away from you, it's gone, and you can't get it back. A few years ago I bought a piano and put it right into a little cubbyhole in my house. I made it pretty public that I was going to start playing again. I told my movie group about it. But when I got ready and sat down, I could not play a thing. It was really gone. I was convinced there was stuff that I remembered that I could really play. But I couldn't do it. I just couldn't do it. I had lost almost everything.

There is always part of me that wonders what would have happened if I had thrown everything into music. I wish I had studied more so I could have written more stuff. If I had learned to read music, it would have made a helluva difference. I probably would have married some great-looking kid.

But I also know that it could have been a tough life. Because in the '50s and '60s big-band music began to die, and a lot of musicians couldn't find work. Even guys like Sinatra struggled for a while when the Big Band Era came to an end. Sinatra needed the movies to finally bring his career back.

There is always part of me that wonders what would have happened if I had thrown everything into music.

I remember walking through an airport one time and coming face to face with Vaughn Monroe. He sang in front of his own band with this rich baritone voice. He had a bunch of hits, such as "Ghost Riders in the Sky." I stopped him and told him how much I enjoyed his band. I mentioned a couple of things like his brass section, which always had eight pieces, and a bridge to a certain song. I could see that I was touching something in him—one musician talking to another. But I also noticed that he was carrying his own bags through the airport trying to get to another job. (Note: Vaughn Monroe died on May 21, 1973).

Another night I was in New York, not far from Madison Square Garden. I walked by this little dive of a club. The door was open, and you could look inside at the band. Sitting there on the drums was the great Gene Krupa, one of the best drummers who ever lived. The guy was obviously on his last legs, just trying to find some kind of job. I never forgot that, because he was so famous and so large, and there he was just trying to hang on.

Maybe something like that would have happened to me if had stuck with music. Who knows?

All I do know is that it wasn't bad riding on that bus with Eugenie Baird.

CHAPTER 4

The War I Could Not Smell

This was taken in 1940 when I was just 18 years old. My neighborhood buddy, Dick Klein, is in the middle. I'm not sure about the guy on the right. Dick and I almost enlisted after Pearl Harbor Day, but his mother put a stop to it.

They sent me for basic training at Camp Maxey, which was about 10 miles north of Paris, Texas. I hadn't been there very long, when somebody, a captain or a colonel, was going through my papers and found the phrase, "Cannot smell. Recommend discharge."

December 7, 1941. If you lived through it, there is no way you will ever forget that day. I remember very clearly the moment I learned that the Japanese had attacked us at Pearl Harbor. I was with my buddy Dick Klein, and after we heard what happened, I started doing everything in my power to get him to enlist with me. I was ready to go because I thought it would be a great adventure. We were so damn young and just looking for excitement. We didn't know anything about war and what it really meant. I was 19 years old.

Dick and I went to the movies that day, and before the movie there was a newsreel. It was about the Japanese attacking somebody else, and when we saw that, knowing what had happened at Pearl Harbor, I kept telling Dick that we needed to go and fight. We nudged each other, thinking that was the

We didn't know anything about war and what it really meant. I was 19 years old.

right thing to do. I was a year older than Dick, and so he was probably going to follow my lead.

We talked about it walking home. We were old enough by the skin of our teeth, and we had already heard about all of these other people who were going to enlist to fight the Japanese. It just seemed like the right thing to do, I guess.

I remember how my father reacted. He sat in the kitchen reading the paper and looking very worried. I heard him say to mom, "Bud will have to go. He'll have to go soon." They talked into the night after I had gone to bed. I could hear them from my room. I didn't pay much attention to the conversation because I had already made up my mind that I wanted to go. And if I was going to go, then Dick wanted to go too.

My father was really mad at the Japanese. The whole country was mad at the Japanese. But at the same time it was hard for me to believe when they opened up those camps on the West Coast to fence those folks in. It certainly was different times. The country was full of young, green people like me and Dick wondering if we should go and fight this fight. We never even considered the possibility that we could die.

Thank God Dick's mother got wind of what we were thinking. She got ahold of him, and the whole thing got stopped. If that didn't happen, we would have gone. I know it. And we would have been killed, sure as hell. We still knew there was a pretty good chance we would get drafted sooner or later, but we didn't go then.

Dick and I had already done a lot of things together. He was a pretty good guitar player, so I would take him along on some music gigs I had.

My dad took him fishing with us one time. I think it was the first time he had ever gone fishing. That son of a gun latched on to one of the biggest walleye pike that anybody caught on that lake all summer. It weighed over 10 pounds, and my dad had to help him get it in. The wind was blowing and blew off Dick's hat. He was more worried about that hat than he was the damned fish. He was worried that his mother would kill him for losing the hat.

I remember one time Dick and I went to the movies, and we got the last two seats in the theater, which were up in the balcony. We sat down in the front row and put our feet over the railing. We both had on loafers, but his were new and didn't fit well. We were looking at the movie, and suddenly Dick's loafers fell off and dropped all the way down into this large crowd of humanity below. He panicked because he was worried about what his mother was going to say. "She'll kill me," Dick kept saying. Dick's mother was a mean horse, and she always thought I was going to be

We were looking at the movie, and suddenly Dick's loafers fell off and dropped all the way down into this large crowd of humanity below.

a bad influence on him. But I liked Dick's dad. I used to go over there on Sunday morning and talk to him when Dick's mother was at church.

Dick and I would get on the streetcar and light our pipes. We would stand in the back of the smoking car and pretend we were men. We would look at the females, but we would never say anything wrong. We didn't have the courage to do that. We were a couple of phonies, that's what we were.

Finally in 1943 I did get drafted, and I left Dick behind because I was a year older. They sent me for basic training at Camp Maxey, which was about 10 miles north of Paris, Texas. I hadn't been there very long, when somebody, a captain or a colonel, was going through my papers and found the phrase, "Cannot smell. Recommend discharge."

That's right. I could not smell anything. Never have been able to. The story I got is that I was two or three years old when my dad and my uncle David were playing with me and tossing me in the air. One of them dropped me right on my face and crushed my nose. And from then on I couldn't smell. So I've never smelled pork chops or pancakes. I know I have missed out on a lot of great smells in my life.

One of them dropped me right on my face and crushed my nose. And from then on I couldn't smell.

I thought they might cut me loose and let me go home immediately. But they kept me around Camp Maxey for a couple of weeks trying to figure out what to do with me. Then one morning at roll call—I remember that it was cold as a dog—they called my name not once but twice.

The officer said, "Private Munson, you've been promoted." Man, was that going to change my life.

I was promoted to a T/5 (Technician, Fifth Grade), which is like a corporal. I was ordered to report to McCloskey General Hospital in

Temple, Texas. My train was leaving in a few hours. They gave me a ticket and said, "You are not to miss that train." They just pulled me right out of there.

I had been assigned to the 69th medical battalion of the 406th Infantry. I was celebrating just getting out of Camp Maxey, when I got on this big, long train. I stood in the smoking car in the back and realized that I was going on this long journey. I had no idea where Temple, Texas, was, but I was convinced that it was going to be a real adventure.

The wounded from the war were flown to San Francisco and then shipped to McCloskey, where they would get surgery. Because I could not smell, they decided to put me in the hospital's recovery room cleaning up the guys who were coming out of surgery. Because when the guys came out of the anesthesia and woke up, it was…blah!!!! They were throwing up all

They were throwing up all around me. I had a towel and a bucket of water, and that was my job.

around me. I had a towel and a bucket of water, and that was my job. It was strange. Blood never bothered me, but that bothered me. That was my contribution to the war effort. I never left Texas.

But I did have time when I was there to put together a helluva band with a great, great sound. We played the clubs around the camps and were starting to do really well. Then one morning I was up on a stage rehearsing with the band, when a sergeant walked in suddenly and told me I was going to be cut loose. I was going home. They had my tickets and everything.

Maybe if I had been older I would have fought to stay and really worked with that band, because it had a great sound. But when that sergeant said "home," all I could think of was Mom and Dad and our house back in Minneapolis. I got my stuff together as quickly as I could and got out of there.

The only memory I have of the trip home to Minnesota was a layover in the Kansas City Airport. I was on a bench sleeping and waiting for my flight, when an MP saw me. Of course I was still in uniform. He whacked me across the bottom of my feet with his nightstick. I don't know if he thought I was AWOL or something, but I had to show him my discharge papers.

I got home and, like I said earlier, there were music jobs all over the place. I did that for a while, and then I made the decision to go to broadcast school. I can't remember exactly where I was, but I'm pretty sure I was in Wyoming when I got the call from my mother.

Dick Klein had been killed in the Philippines. He was a spotter on an artillery-spotting plane during the Battle of Mindanao.

It popped me hard. Early in the war one of the older guys in the neighborhood, Bill Larsen, was killed. I didn't know him well. But Dick and I had spent so much time together as kids. We used to sit in his front yard on a steep bank and talk about what we were going to do with our lives. We *Somebody I grew up with, played with, and had dreams with. He was gone, and I was still alive.* both loved music. We talked about making it in music together. We had some growing-up adventures.

My mom went to the funeral home. She said that she didn't recognize Dick because he had gained a bunch of weight.

At the time I just couldn't understand it. Somebody I grew up with, played with, and had dreams with. He was gone, and I was still alive. I asked myself why.

After all we had been through together, of all places, he went down in an artillery plane in the Philippines.

And, by God, that made him a man.

CHAPTER 5

Coming Home,
Moving On

Curt Gowdy gave me my first real job when he hired me to replace him in Cheyenne, Wyoming. We became lifelong friends. PHOTO COURTESY OF AP IMAGES

Well, to me that sounded like the worst damn thing in the world. I was young, and you couldn't tell me anything because I knew it all.
I finally got to the point where I didn't talk to them any more about it. When my temporary job at Ford was over, I just walked out the door.

W hen I got home from the service, there were jobs all over the place because so many men were in the war. There was plenty of music work, and I did a lot of touring. But if I wasn't going to make music my career I had to figure out what I was going to do with my life.

I got a temporary job at the Ford Motor Company in St. Paul test-driving and working with the M8 armored car. At some point during the war the military decided they needed to go to a lighter, quicker armored vehicle. What I heard was that our Sherman tank could not stack up against the German Panzers, particularly in the sand. The Germans had cleaned our clocks in a couple of tank battles in Africa, so the Ford Motor Company was supposed to deliver hundreds of these M8 things as quickly as they could.

The M8 did not have a tread like conventional tanks. It had big, thick tires. It could hold four men inside, and because it was lighter, it could go something like 64 miles per hour.

They put me in one of those things to drive it, and man it could really go. And when I climbed out of that tank everybody was watching me. I really got caught up in it because it made me feel special.

In order to ship these things out of the factory, they had to be lifted up by a crane with four hooks, one on each corner. The crane would lift them up and swing them out wide and put them on a flatbed railroad car. There were slots in the flatbed for the wheels. That is where I came in. I helped get those hooks in place and swing the M8 into position. I got hit by those hooks several times, getting a few black eyes.

I got hit by those hooks several times, getting a few black eyes.

One time the thing got me good and broke all of the fingers in my right hand. It just bent the whole hand backward, and they had to lay me off for six weeks.

Ford eventually called me back and gave me a job painting with my one good hand. It was during that time that one of the foremen came to me and wanted to talk. They were going to offer me a permanent job. In fact, they said that after the war they expected to be very busy, and if I came with Ford full-time they would promise to make me a foreman down the road.

At the time I didn't know exactly what all was involved in a job like that, but it sounded like it would probably be a really good thing. I told my old man about it, and he got excited. He looked up the retirement plan and everything involved. He said, "You should take this, Bud. You don't want to do insurance [like me]."

Dad said he knew people who had been working at Ford all of their lives. It was a great job with a great future, he said. My sister was pushing me also, because it was a good job with good security. She said it sounded good.

Well, to me that sounded like the worst damn thing in the world. I was young, and you couldn't tell me anything because I knew it all. I finally got to the point where I didn't talk to them any more about it. When my temporary job at Ford was over, I just walked out the door. I didn't know what I was going to do with my life, but I wasn't going to spend it working at the Ford Motor Company.

I didn't know what I was going to do with my life, but I wasn't going to spend it working at the Ford Motor Company.

Then one day I was walking down the street and heard this advertisement blaring from a radio. The ad said that because of the war there was a shortage of radio broadcasters all over the country. If you came to their broadcasting school they would teach you everything you needed to know, and they would guarantee you a job. They said to bring your discharge check, which for me was $200, and they would do the rest.

They said that the broadcast school would be about 20 or so weeks, but after about the 11th week they found a job for me out in Devils Lake, North Dakota, reading the news. That is where the radio school sent me. I had to borrow a trunk from my sister to go all the way out there.

The very first day I was there, I had to do the news at 6:45 AM. I had never been on the air in my life. But the husband and wife who owned the little station showed me how to cut up the audio and get it ready to go on the air.

So I was ready to do my very first broadcast. And while I was waiting to go on the air, I saw this white figure move in front of me like a ghost. It turned out that the husband and wife had their bedroom right next to the studio. She got up early to go to the bathroom, and right as I started talking she flushed the toilet, and I damned near died laughing right

And while I was waiting to go on the air, I saw this white figure move in front of me like a ghost.

on the air. I don't remember her name, but I do remember that the nightgown was ugly.

I was only there for two weeks, because I wanted to do sports. I found out about a job in Cheyenne, Wyoming, where Curt Gowdy was calling University of Wyoming football and basketball. Gowdy was going to Oklahoma City to work for Hank Iba, Oklahoma State's great basketball coach, and to do minor-league baseball. He wanted me to take his place at Wyoming. I put together an audition tape of a fake game between Ohio State and Michigan with all kinds of fake sound effects. I got the job, and it was off to Wyoming.

Gowdy became a great friend, and we did a lot of fun things together. Through Gowdy I got a chance to meet people like Ted Williams. I had a good long talk with him once, and he gave me some great Gowdy stories. But I remember that every other word was the F-word.

One time after Gowdy started doing the Yankees, he and I spent part of our vacation together down in St. Petersburg during spring training. Every night it seemed Casey Stengel would get shit-faced in one of the local bars and just stand around and tell baseball stories. I was really lucky to be on the outskirts of that crowd and get to listen.

Every night it seemed Casey Stengel would get shit-faced in one of the local bars and just stand around and tell baseball stories.

However, my wife at the time didn't think it was too interesting.

Wyoming was a lot of fun because there was already a great basketball tradition when I got there. They had won the national championship in 1943 with a pair of great All-Americans, Kenny Sailors and Milo Komenich. Wyoming had become a national program, and they traveled all over by train. This was a big-time bunch.

Sailors wasn't a big guy, only 5'10", but he was known as the man who invented the jump shot. He was an All-American in 1942 and 1943 and then went off to the war like the rest of us. He came back for the 1946 season. He was again an All-American, and Wyoming won the conference championship.

Komenich was a real character. He was an Indiana guy who played on the national championship team and also came back after the war. The guy was really built and good-looking. In fact, he tried out for Tarzan. We were out in California, and a movie studio out there was looking for the new Tarzan. They invited him to audition and invited the whole team to come along. That was a helluva mistake. It would have been a great deal for the kid if he had gotten the part. But when we got there they had stripped him down and put a leopard skin on him with a knife in his belt. They gave him a girl

My boyhood home in Minnesota, complete with snow. The clothes-line on the right was my goalpost where I practiced kicking field goals.

Mom and Dad at home after a successful pheasant hunt. Mom didn't shoot, but she was a good sport to pose for the pictures.

Mom visiting friends at a little cabin on the lake. She was always cooking something.

My dad, Harry, was the best fish-cleaner I have ever seen. I learned everything I know about hunting and fishing from him.

My sister Dorothy (who we all called Dot) and I in December 1932. I was 10, and she was 12. We used to fight like cats and dogs.

Dot loved to fish as much as I did.

Here I am with the whole family in 1933 as we celebrate my grandparents' 50th wedding anniversary. I'm the good-looking one kneeling on the left. I was 11 years old.

One year in Nashville I wrote a fishing guide. I didn't make any money, but I had some fun.

Every Sunday morning, regardless of where we would play on Saturday, I was out in the boat shooting film for my weekly fishing show.

There was nothing I enjoyed more than catching my limit. With all those lakes around Nashville, it was easy to do.

This is my 16 mm camera I used to shoot film for my hunting and fishing show in Nashville. The damn thing weighed a ton.

I hosted a college football preview show in Nashville. This one was on September 21, 1956. On my right is Peter Gracey, a former player at Vanderbilt. On my left is Georgia SID Dan Magill. He was there because Vanderbilt played Georgia the next day. PHOTO COURTESY OF THE UNIVERSITY OF GEORGIA

One of the sponsors of our baseball broadcasts in Nashville sold hot dogs. He got me to pose for this crazy shot.

Sulphur Dell was the oldest minor-league baseball park in the country when the final game was played there in 1963.

After I lost the Braves job in 1967 I returned to Nashville to work in local TV again. It was tough going back.

Munson Power available to you on a daily basis

MUNSON'S SPORTS EDITORIALS

TO YOUR AUDIENCE   TO YOUR STATION   TO YOUR SPONSOR

MUNSON POWER MEANS...

- Hard-hitting Commentary
- Incisive Reporting
- Penetrating Analysis
- Behind "Closed-Door" Research
- Humorous "Hit-'Em-In-The-Gut" Style

- Instant Audience Appeal
- Massive Sales Appeal
- Flexible Programming Format
- Strong Audience Comment, Mail Pull

- Immediate Listener Interest
- Exclusive Showcase For Image-Building Commercials
- Excellent Merchandising, Cross Promotion Advantages
- Fresh, New Shows Everyday, Monday thru Friday, 260 Times A Year

I interviewed O.J. Simpson in the Nashville airport after he did a Hertz commercial.

to work off of. God, the guys were just on the floor. We just butchered the test for him.

Wyoming had a pretty famous coach named Ev Shelton. (Note: Everett Shelton was the head basketball coach at Wyoming from 1939 to 1959.) He was known throughout the country. They told Shelton to take me to a room and diagram his offense. They drove me from Cheyenne to Laramie, which was about 55 miles, and I sat down with Ev Shelton. He was just like a teacher, giving me the correct, clinical pronunciation of every term. They wanted to make damn sure I knew what he was talking about. It was quite an education, I'll tell you that.

But Gowdy always told me that the only way I was going to ever make any money in radio was to get involved in baseball. That's what he did. He was only in Oklahoma a couple of years before he became Mel Allen's partner on the New York Yankees broadcast. Then he went on to be the No. 1 guy for the Boston Red Sox. That is what I wanted to do.

But Gowdy always told me that the only way I was going to ever make any money in radio was to get involved in baseball.

Wyoming was a great place to start, but in order to do baseball I knew I was going to have to move.

I had grown up loving big-band music. Little did I know that my next big break would come in the country music capital of the world.

CHAPTER 6

Nashville: Vanderbilt and Sulphur Dell

Calling minor-league baseball for the Nashville Vols at Sulphur Dell, one of the oldest ballparks in the country. With me is my engineer, Big John.

The radio management
came to my house
and suspended me immediately.
I know they were worried about
their license getting snatched
plus some kind of fine
from the FCC.
They put out a letter that
made it seem like I was fired.

On January 5, 1947, WKDA Radio in Nashville was born, and I was the first sports director. I had moved to Nashville in December on Gowdy's advice. I finally got a baseball job calling the Nashville Vols minor-league team. I was also set to work Vanderbilt football and basketball. I thought it was a pretty good deal. Little did I know that I would stay for 20 years.

I loved working for that station. Because of my background in music they let me buy the albums that we would play on the air. I remember going through record bins in the stores in Nashville and pulling out those old 78s. We played a lot of Sinatra and Nat King Cole.

Minor-league baseball was big back then. The Vols played in this old ballpark called Sulphur Dell, which got the name because it had an old sulphur spring running underneath it. Some days when it was really hot I was told that the smell was terrible. I couldn't smell it, but that is what the people would tell me.

I remember going through record bins in the stores in Nashville and pulling out those old 78s.

As much as I loved it, minor-league baseball almost got me fired from the radio for good. It was a Sunday afternoon doubleheader in 1948, and the Vols were playing in New Orleans. Back then the radio guys rarely traveled with the team. We just used the Western Union wire in the studio to get the information and then broadcast it like we were live. We would use sound effects to get the sound of the crack of the bat and the crowd noise. I would hit the microphone with a pencil for the crack of the bat. I would have to do a lot of research, because all I got from Western Union was whether the pitch was a ball or a strike and how the out was made. I had to fill in the details myself. It seems crazy to talk about that now, because you could never get away with it. But back then that is what we did to save money.

I don't know if I was getting bored or what. I thought my microphone was off. I was trying to get the attention of my engineer, who was definitely bored, because he was reading a magazine. So I just blurted out, "This is really a fucking way to make a living, huh?"

The engineer stuck his head up and looked at me in absolute horror.

The engineer stuck his head up and looked at me in absolute horror. He looked down at the microphone switch, then I looked down as well. The microphone was hot, and I knew I was in trouble.

The radio management came to my house and suspended me immediately. I know they were worried about their license getting snatched plus some kind of fine from the FCC. They put out a letter that made it seem like I was fired.

A minister over in Murfreesboro was getting ready to put together a petition to get me out of there. But Fred Russell, the great writer and sports editor from the *Nashville Banner,* found that minister and got that thing stopped. It took about a week to calm everybody down. I was close to getting railroaded out of there, but I got back on the air.

Nashville is also where I started my hunting and fishing show, which we called *The Rod and Gun Club.* When I started there were only a handful of people doing hunting and fishing shows, and nobody was taking a camera out on the weekend and shooting film. I eventually moved to WSM, the big radio station in Nashville, and there I had a chance to get to know some of the country and western singing stars in town. Some of them came on the show as my guests. Porter Wagoner was a big fisherman, and Jerry Reed loved to fish for small-mouth bass. We would fish at a place called Percy Priest Lake in Nashville. A bunch of the backup musicians were part of that show.

I loved Nashville, but I really had to hustle to make a living. I remember having to get a job in a sporting-goods store where all the country-music people would shop. I was in charge of all of the hunting and fishing stuff, and at Christmas the wives of all these singers would come in there and tell me what they wanted to get their husbands. And then I would take care of it. You talk about busy! I really liked that job.

One night I was at a cocktail party, and I thought I was about to get the break of my career. F.M. Williams, a writer for the *Tennessean* newspaper, pulled me into a corner. Gowdy had just left the Yankees to become the No.1 guy for the Boston Red Sox radio team. Williams had talked to Mel Allen, and according to Williams, Allen said he had just hired Larry Munson to replace Gowdy. F.M. just jumped on it because he thought he had the story of the night. He came to me and asked if it was true, and I had to say that I didn't know. I hadn't heard anything about it. I heard later that the Yankees front office had decided that they were going to make the call. So if Mel Allen really wanted me, they killed it.

One night I was at a cocktail party, and I thought I was about to get the break of my career.

When I started working Vanderbilt basketball I tried to convince the officials there that Vanderbilt's program could be just as good as Wyoming's. But they didn't give out scholarships in basketball, and they didn't have a place to play. Vanderbilt would play at high schools around town. It was pretty bad. But then Vanderbilt hired Bob Polk as coach. Polk signed a bunch of really good players. Some of them were guys from Indiana that Kentucky and Indiana didn't want, but they were good. When I got there Vanderbilt had only one guy on scholarship, a great local player from Nashville named Billy Joe Adcock. He would become the first All-America basketball player ever at Vanderbilt.

My boss in Nashville was a Vanderbilt alum named Tom Baker. Tom would eventually lead the drive to build Memorial Gym. Like I said, Vanderbilt was playing in local high schools when I got there, and then they ended up playing at McQuiddy Gym over at David Lipscomb University. They finally got Memorial Gym built in 1952, and it meant all the difference in the world.

There are so many basketball memories:

♦ In 1951 Vanderbilt beat Kentucky to win the SEC Tournament. But that year the regular-season champion got to go to the NCAA tournament. Vanderbilt stayed home, and Kentucky won the national championship.

♦ In 1961 we finished tied for second in the league with Kentucky. Mississippi State won the SEC, but their state legislature didn't want them to play in the NCAA tournament because of the racial thing. (Note: The Mississippi legislature prevented the 1961 Mississippi State basketball team from playing in the NCAA tournament because the opposing teams in the tournament would have had African American players.) So we had to go to Knoxville to play Kentucky to see who would get the NCAA tournament bid. Kentucky filled up that Tennessee field house. And of course that Kentucky band was there making all that noise. We didn't have a band. We knew we were dead when they hit the floor. We would have rather played in Lexington, where we usually played pretty good. (Note: Kentucky won 88–67 and advanced to the NCAA tournament.)

♦ In 1965 I got as close to the Final Four as I was ever going to get. We had a great team that year with Clyde Lee, who was an All-America center, and John Ed Miller. Roy Skinner was the coach. Vanderbilt won the SEC with a 23–3 record—15–1 in the SEC—and got a bid to the NCAA tournament. We went to the Mideast regional in Lexington, Kentucky. Michigan, Dayton, and

DePaul were also there. We beat DePaul 83–78 in overtime and advanced to the championship against Michigan. Michigan had a great team with Cazzie Russell. John Ed Miller kept us in it with his shooting, but he got trapped, and they called him for walking with about 15 seconds left. Michigan won 87–85. It was a helluva game.

I remember that before the game Michigan had left their locker-room door open. As I walked by I looked inside. On the blackboards were the words *Destroy* and *Kill.*

That was the same day I interviewed Perry Wallace, the black kid out of Pearl High School in Nashville, who would later become the first African American basketball player at Vanderbilt. He was a bright young kid, and I enjoyed talking

> *As I walked by I looked inside. On the blackboards were the words* Destroy *and* Kill.

to him. We only talked about four or five minutes, but some of the die-hard alumni really resented that I did that. They called the station. They called my house. I never understood that.

SEC basketball was so different back then. Adolph Rupp of Kentucky basically controlled the league. He would clash with the referees all the time and always seemed to get his way. I can still hear that shrill voice of his screaming.

Then there was Ray Mears of Tennessee. We all hated Mears so much. He was such a basketball showman. They said he was getting the older AAU players from Ohio that Vanderbilt couldn't get.

The basketball arenas in the league were just awful. I remember going to Woodruff at Georgia, where they had a popcorn machine in the corner that made too much noise. Florida had "Alligator Alley," where the students were right on top of you. They were some of the worst of the bunch.

In 1957 we went on the road to play Penn State in football. Joe Paterno was still an assistant. (Note: Paterno became the head coach at Penn State in 1966.) Nobody gave us a chance, but we won the damn game. They had us 20–6 at halftime, but Judd Collins, the color man on our broadcast, said to me, "Hell, we're going to beat them." And in the second half we started throwing short all over the place and came back to beat them 32–20. What I remember most about that trip was driving back to Harrisburg to catch the flight home. We flew over the steel mills of Pittsburgh, and it was about 11:00 PM. It was an impressive sight. The pilot told everybody to move over to the right side of the plane so that they could see the fire coming out of the steel mills. But when all of those football players shifted to one side, the plane jumped in that direction, and the pilot had to correct it and guys had to scramble back to the other side. I never forgot that and the sight of those steel mills.

There was another football trip to UCLA, in 1961. I remember that the night before the game the music industry invited us to see the *Lawrence Welk Show*. The driver of the bus announced that he was going to show us something special.

He took us to the top of a hill in Los Angeles, and down below we saw about 100 million lights coming at us.

He took us to the top of a hill in Los Angeles, and down below we saw about 100 million lights coming at us. The driver said, "You are looking at one of the new things coming to America. You are looking at what they call an expressway."

All we could see was bumper-to-bumper cars with all of these people trying to get home. Man, that was really something.

Earlier that day a bunch of the TV and newspaper guys got an invitation to play golf with Lawrence Welk. I stayed behind and enjoyed some time in the pool at the Biltmore Hotel. I was in the pool treading water, and I found myself looking up at an extremely well-known television star—Lorne Greene from *Bonanza*. All I know is that there were a lot of pretty women around him. I knew I was close to Hollywood.

Nashville was just a great place to live. I really loved doing the hunting and fishing show, even though it was a grind and I didn't make a lot of money. I had really built it into something. I also enjoyed working in the SEC with Vanderbilt. By the '60s minor-league baseball was really starting to die, but I still enjoyed it.

I was in the pool treading water, and I found myself looking up at an extremely well-known television star— Lorne Greene from Bonanza.

But there was part of me that wondered what it would be like to do Major League Baseball like Gowdy. Was I ever going to get that chance? And if I did, would I want to leave Nashville?

In 1966 both of those questions were finally answered.

CHAPTER 7

The Braves: Big Break, Big Heartache

Here I am interviewing Willie McCovey of the Giants during my two years (1966–1967) with the Atlanta Braves. I thought I was set for life when I got the Braves job, but Milo Hamilton had other plans.

Once the season starts,
baseball is a grind,
no doubt about it.
There are a lot of games
and a lot of travel.
You are gone for long periods
at the time.
But there is also a lot
of laughter in baseball.

The Gardner Advertising Agency out of St. Louis was able to hear me because I was doing the minor-league Vols on WSM in Nashville, which was a 50,000-watt station. By the mid-1960s minor-league baseball had become a dying situation. Attendance was down. People started staying at home and doing other things. It was pretty obvious that there was not going to be a future in minor-league baseball.

The Gardner Agency offered me the job of joining the new Braves team as they went to Atlanta from Milwaukee. I kept thinking about what Gowdy had told me. He said I would never make any real money in radio unless I got involved in baseball, like he did, by calling the major leagues.

Believe it or not, it was a tough decision. I was going to have to pull up stakes and go, leaving everything I had done in Nashville behind. I had built that hunting and fishing show into something pretty good. I wasn't making a ton of money doing it, but I was proud of the show. I loved the damned thing. I never told a lot of people this, but I thought about backing out of the Braves thing at the last minute, but I couldn't do it. It was a job in Major League Baseball, and I just couldn't turn that down.

All of a sudden I was in a car driving to spring training in West Palm Beach and a totally different life.

So they took Milo Hamilton, who was the No. 2 guy with the Chicago White Sox, and me, a minor-league announcer. All of a sudden I was in a car driving to spring training in West Palm Beach and a totally different life.

There is nothing like your first time at spring training in the major leagues. The only time we would broadcast spring-training games was on the weekend, so during the week all we had to do was interview two ballplayers around the 10:00 hour. We would just drive to the ballpark, and the engineer would be there waiting for us. They wanted us to interview players from other teams. I'll never forget that my first interview down there was with Bill Mazeroski of the Pirates. Somebody else had set it up, all I had to do was do the interview, and somebody else would feed it down the line. After that we usually headed for the golf course.

And the golf courses down in West Palm Beach that time of year were incredible. The grass was so green. The water was so blue. The sand was so white. My work was done for the day, and then I was on the golf course. I kept asking myself, *My God, how could anything be this easy?* We would have so much fun teaching Joe Torre, our catcher, how to play. He would hit this incredible slice, so we would aim him about 111 yards out to the left. Man, would we laugh.

Once the season starts, baseball is a grind, no doubt about it.

There were so many great times with the Braves and so many great memories.

There are a lot of games and a lot of travel. You are gone for long periods at the time. But there is also a lot of laughter in baseball. There were so many great times with the Braves and so many great memories.

There were a lot of amazing players on that first Braves team in 1966: Hank Aaron, Felipe Alou, Eddie Mathews, Joe Torre, Rico Carty. It seemed like we would get off to a good start and then kind of fall apart. (Note: The 1966 Braves finished 85–77 and finished fifth in the National League. By June 3 the Braves were 10 games under .500 at 20–30.)

There were so many personalities on that team. Aaron was such a proud man and so damned talented. Torre was our jokester and a great hitter. But he did like the nightlife, and downtown Atlanta was a pretty wild place back then. Felipe Alou spoke in broken English, but he was handsome and very popular with the ladies. Alou was a good guy, and everybody liked working with him. I liked Mack Jones too, but he had a temper.

Little Donald Davidson was the traveling secretary and a great, great baseball man. We had such fun with him.

When we would travel back then we would always have the two stalwarts of the Atlanta newspapers—Jesse Outlar and Furman Bisher—with us. They were the best. They knew their stuff, and the players respected them.

We would pass the time before we would head to the ballpark by going to movies. Ernie Johnson and a reporter from the *AJC*, Wayne Minshew, would go with me to one movie at 11:00 AM and sometimes another one at 1:30 PM. I always enjoyed their company.

I remember the day that Tony Cloninger, a pitcher, hit those two grand slams in San Francisco (on Sunday, July 3, 1966). Cloninger was this big, strong guy from North Carolina, and back then he was hitting everything that was thrown at him. I remember Cloninger sitting at breakfast every morning on the road with a bunch of the players who had gone to college. They weren't talking about baseball. They had out the morning paper and were talking about the stock market.

Paul Richards was the general manager of the Braves, and he was a pretty straight-down-the-line kind of guy. I remember when Clete Boyer joined the team at third base after we traded Eddie Mathews to the Houston Astros prior to the 1967 season. Richards found out that they were going to put Boyer and Torre together in the same room on the road. Man, that upset Richards, because he knew both those guys liked to have a good time.

I remember taking my two adopted kids down to the first spring training, and they got out there with the players trying to shag flies. Richards really blew his stack over that.

Man, that upset Richards, because he knew both those guys liked to have a good time.

When you finally get a major-league job, you figure you're going to do it for the rest of your life. I had the Braves, and later, in 1966,

I got Georgia football. At that point I pretty much had what I wanted as a broadcaster. I would have been happy doing the Braves and Georgia football from then on. But it didn't work out that way.

At the end of the first season there were a lot of rumors flying around that the Braves were going to change announcers. And once we got into the second season there were signs all around, if I had just paid attention to them. It became clear to me that Milo Hamilton wanted me out, and eventually he succeeded.

It became clear to me and Milo Hamilton wanted me out, and eventually he succeeded.

The best thing I can say about Milo is that he was very difficult to get along with. I always got the sense that he expected people to bow down to him. Sometimes in spring training we would go to a movie and go play golf, and we would laugh like we were real buddies. And then we would go to the ballpark, and he would shut it down. He would literally turn his back on me. He would act like I didn't exist. The game, the fans, everything was about him.

He was trying to get me out from the day I got there. He was talented, but he wasn't a play-by-play guy. But God, he had a voice—an incredible voice.

We would play golf with Ernie Johnson, who was a helluva golfer and a helluva nice man, and Torre, who was always a lot of fun and was trying to learn how to play the game the right way. We had some other good golfers on the team, such as Dick Kelley and Wade Blasingame, our left-handed pitchers. But Milo would screw those afternoons up, too, because of his temper.

I remember when the soccer team, the Atlanta Chiefs, came along and they needed somebody to do the games. There wasn't any money in it, but I had to do it because Milo wouldn't touch it. Then they put together a big publicity trip to London for the team. I looked up, and Milo was going and I wasn't. So I had to raise a little hell about that. He wasn't even doing the damn games, and he talked himself onto the trip.

So we both ended up going to London, and they put us in the same room together. I didn't know how that was going to work out, but it turned out to be a decent trip. Milo and I had some laughs. We actually had some fun together. But when the games started, it was the same thing. It was like I didn't exist. The guy just had one helluva ego.

Milo even managed to make Hank Aaron mad. In 1967 he was at the All-Star Game luncheon in Atlanta and stood up to introduce Roberto Clemente, the great Pittsburgh right fielder. In so many words Milo said that *Milo even managed* Clemente had beaten out Aaron as the All-Star *to make Hank* right fielder. (Note: In reality Aaron had received *Aaron mad.* more All-Star votes than any National League outfielder. He only played left field in the All-Star Game because he was asked to do so by National League manager Walter Alston.)

Aaron was so mad after what Milo said that the rest of the Braves players put out the word that no media, including him, should come to the locker room like they normally did before the game. In fact, Milo called me and asked me to do his pregame player interviews that day. Everybody thought it was going to get into a big confrontation, but it never got to that. Aaron stayed mad at Milo for a long time.

At the end of the 1967 season I got the sense that the Braves knew it was a divided house and that they might just blow both of us out. But Milo was smart. He had an agent, and the agent was meeting with the Braves and convincing them that Milo needed another guy in the other chair. Milo put out a lot of stuff that I didn't know anything about baseball. I was old enough—older than him—to hold onto my temper. But it was not an easy thing to do. I should have just plowed in there and told the Braves how I felt, but I didn't bother to do it at all.

The bottom line with Milo was that he was always trying to feed his own ego. He needed to have the recognition. I'm guessing that he thought he was the greatest announcer in the world and that nobody belonged with him. He couldn't stand any kind of semi-decent publicity for anybody else—especially the guy sitting next to him.

When the Braves finally let me go, Milo wanted everybody to think that he had made the change. Did he actually make it? It really didn't matter, because the change had been made. Milo finally got his way after two years, and I was out of there. I remember when the guy from the Braves told me they were going to make a change. I told him, "You mean I'm out and that son of a bitch has survived?"

For a long time I was pissed at the Braves and the fact that Milo may have had something to do with me being let go. It was especially hard to take after so many people had been telling me that I was doing a good job. I didn't argue with anybody. There were things in my contract that said I wasn't supposed to criticize the club on the air. So I found myself trying to pull back a little so as not to step on the company's toes. And it struck me that the other guy was not holding back anything.

I really enjoyed baseball. I had spent so many years with that minor-league club in Nashville, and I thought I would do the same in the major leagues. I had a couple of major-league jobs cross my path after that. The White Sox came after me pretty hard one year, and I almost took it. It was combined with Northwestern football and basketball, and those teams had not had very much success. So I eventually turned that one down.

The White Sox came after me pretty hard one year, and I almost took it.

I was living in Lenox Square Apartments in Atlanta when the Braves let me go. I had just knocked out the wall and taken the unit next door, and I was going to fix it up really nice. But now all I had in my hand was Georgia football, and that didn't pay a whole lot. We were in the third game of the year, and so it was just a shock.

So eventually I had to go back to Nashville and try to put the fishing show back together in order to make a living. I had left Nashville in 1966 with a party and everything because of this great opportunity with the Braves. Now I was going to have to go back and eat crow. That was hard. Man, that was hard.

Now I was going to have to go back and eat crow.

But I still had Georgia. I didn't know it at the time, but 40 years later I would still have Georgia.

CHAPTER 8

The '60s:
At Last a Bulldog!

LARRY MUNSON
Voice of Bulldogs

Munson Selected New 'Dog 'Voice'

Larry Munson, who recently moved from Nashville to Atlanta to broadcast Braves baseball, will be the play-by-play announcer of University of Georgia football games in 1966, Bulldog Athletic Director Joel Eaves announced Saturday.

The lanky, crew-cut Munson, a Minnesota native who was voted Tennessee's No. 1 sportscaster the past four years, succeeds Ed Thilenius as voice-of-the-Bulldogs. Thilenius has gone to the Atlanta Falcons' broadcasting network.

Munson broadcast Nashville Vol baseball 14 years, Vanderbilt basketball 16 years and football 10 years. He was sports director of Nashville WSM.

I was 43 years old when I got the Georgia job in 1966. I was still holding on to that crewcut. PHOTO COURTESY OF THE UNIVERSITY OF GEORGIA

*He asked Dan if he had ever
heard me do a game.
Dan said he had heard me
do basketball and liked it.
"Good," Joel told Dan.
"I just hired him.
You can tell the media."*

I said that when I took the Braves job in 1966 I literally had to pick up everything and move. I was told to go to Atlanta and pick up a rental car there that would have my name on it. I was to get the car and drive to such-and-such hotel in West Palm Beach. And there would be a hotel room waiting on me, where I would stay for 31 days.

I took everything with me—fishing gear, old clothes, everything—because I had been told about those 31 straight days in a hotel. I got to the car place in Atlanta, which I believe was over on Spring Street. I picked up an Atlanta newspaper out of a box on the street, threw it in the car, and then I headed to West Palm Beach. I think I got there about 11 hours later.

By that point it was 2:00 AM. I checked into the Holiday Inn. When I got into the room I started putting all of my stuff—fishing gear and guns—back into the corner of the closet where nobody would see it. I took the newspaper—which I hadn't looked at yet—and threw it on the bed. I decided to take a shower, and after that I finally looked at the copy of the *Atlanta Journal*.

When I got into the room I started putting all of my stuff—fishing gear and guns—back into the corner of the closet where nobody would see it.

There was a little box on the front page that Ed Thilenius, who had been doing radio for Georgia football, had turned in his notice. He was going to do the Falcons on Channel 5 in Atlanta. In the story, Joel Eaves, the Georgia athletic director, said he was going to start taking applications for his job. I couldn't believe it.

I had known Joel Eaves for a long, long time. I first got to know him when he was the head basketball coach at Auburn (from 1950 to 1963). He was a very successful coach, and at Vanderbilt we had played a lot of big games against him. I was also interested in Eaves because his offense was the Drake Shuffle, which was basically the same offense we were running at Vanderbilt. I liked to exchange notes with him.

In fact, Eaves would come to scout Vanderbilt games at Memorial Gym. And because there was really no good place for a scout to sit, I would let him sit in the radio booth with me and the engineer. You could see the game so much better from up there. And at halftime I would put him on the air, and he would break down the entire game for us. He did that several times, and so we got kind of close.

So the next morning I called Joel before I went down to breakfast and told him that I was very interested in the Georgia job. He never hesitated. Because he knew me and wanted someone with experience in the SEC, he took me right there on the phone.

And just like that I was the voice of the Georgia Bulldogs.

And just like that I was the voice of the Georgia Bulldogs. I didn't know what to expect, but I was pretty excited.

I found out later that as soon as Joel hired me he went and found Dan Magill, the Georgia sports information director. He asked Dan if he had ever heard me do a game. Dan said he had heard me do basketball and liked it. "Good," Joel told Dan. "I just hired him. You can tell the media." (Note: Dan Magill confirmed this story.)

I couldn't get to Athens to talk to people right then because of baseball season and my commitment to the Braves. But the fact that I had the Georgia job made that first season in baseball easier for me when I began to figure out what a blankety-blank Milo was going to be.

But I did make one mistake during that time. When I left Nashville to take the Braves job, I just basically left the folks at Vanderbilt on hold. I would not commit to the radio station in Nashville that I was going to come back to do Vanderbilt. I didn't treat them well. I should have given them my word that I was coming back. I was trying to cover myself in case the baseball thing didn't work out. I should have promised to take the Vanderbilt job one more year, but I didn't. I just walked away from them. I really didn't play that right.

What I knew about Georgia football was from my days at Vanderbilt. I knew Georgia had a young coach in Vince Dooley and that he was a pretty bright guy. Georgia had been a pretty good team under Wally Butts (from 1939 to 1960) but had slipped after he left.

When you get to be my age, some of the seasons kind of run together. But there are some pretty good memories of my first few seasons at Georgia in the 1960s.

I never dreamed that we would win a championship in 1966, my first season. It was Dooley's third year, and he felt pretty good about the talent after a couple of years of pretty good recruiting. I remember that our first game was against Mississippi State in Jackson, and we had to fight like a dog to get out of

I never dreamed that we would win a championship in 1966, my first season.

there alive with a 20–17 win. I remember that we lost a tough one to Miami 7–6 down there. That would be the only one we lost.

We played against Steve Spurrier right at the end of his career at Florida. Our guys got after him pretty good. Georgia won 27–10, but Spurrier went on to win the Heisman Trophy. And I do remember going over to Auburn and winning a tough, tough game on the road 21–13. Things were so different back then. I remember getting on the bus with the team after the Auburn game. Then the captain, George Patton, came on and congratulated the whole team on being the SEC champions. Everybody let out this big roar. I remember thinking, *My God! I've already won an SEC title.* (Note: In 1966 Georgia and Alabama tied at 6–0 in the SEC and shared the conference championship.)

Georgia went to the Cotton Bowl after that season, but I couldn't go because the broadcasts of the bowl games were sponsored by Texaco. Texaco had a rule that the radio announcers could not work any game in which their team was playing. But Texaco did send me to a bunch of other bowl games every year, such as the Gator, Sun, Cotton, and Liberty Bowls. It was a pretty good deal. We would travel with the Texaco guy to each city, and he would take us out to dinner.

Back in the 1950s and early 1960s the radio guys were really treated well because television had really not caught on for college football. But I remember when things began to change. We were flying to El Paso to do the Sun Bowl with the Texaco guy, Dick Frick, who was the head of all their advertising. We were sitting up in first class. The TV guys from NBC were sitting back in the plane, in coach.

But when we got to El Paso the chamber of commerce guys went straight to the TV people and made out like they were heroes. We were pretty steamed about that. We thought it was pretty lousy to make heroes out of those guys and ignore us. But Frick got us in the cab and told us not to worry. He said college football on television wasn't really going to catch on; it wasn't going to mean anything.

He said college football on television wasn't really going to catch on; it wasn't going to mean anything.

going to catch on; it wasn't going to mean anything. Then, as we were riding, he showed us a big mall with all those cars. That, he said, was going to be our audience—people in their cars. Because of that, TV would not be a factor. I liked Dick, but I guess you could say that he was wrong about that.

In 1968 we opened at Tennessee and thought we might have a helluva team. Jake Scott was on that team. So was Bill Stanfill. We thought Stanfill was huge, but by today's standards he would be average. But he was a great defensive end. We went to Knoxville, and the entire discussion about that game was that it was going to be played on artificial turf. Tennessee was the first school in the conference to put that stuff in, and nobody had any idea what it was going to be like. I just remember that Erk Russell, Georgia's defensive coordinator, was really concerned about it. Dooley wasn't real thrilled about it either because we didn't know how hot it was going to be on the damned rug or if we would be able to stand up on the thing. We ended up in a 17–17 tie when Tennessee scored right at the end. That was a big moment in the conference because a number of other schools got the rug after that. I just remember that Erk didn't like it and didn't want to play on it again.

But that wasn't the first game that we had ever played on AstroTurf. The year before, in 1967, we went to Houston and played in the Astrodome in one of the first college football games ever played on the stuff. I will always remember pulling up to that huge Astrodome, and there were shoe salesmen all over the place. They were offering shoes to the team, because they were trying to get their shoes in that game. Houston was ranked and really well known, and we had a helluva game with them. (Note: Houston defeated Georgia 15–14 on November 4, 1967, in Houston.)

I will always remember pulling up to that huge Astrodome, and there were shoe salesmen all over the place.

The next year we played Houston in Athens, and boy did they have some studs! They were averaging over 500 yards a game, and they were running up and down the field on us. But our defense held them to only one touchdown. We were undefeated, but late in the game we still trailed 10–7. Then our quarterback, Mike Cavan, got us on a little drive late, and Jim McCullough kicked a field goal to tie the game 10–10. It felt like we had won, because Houston had a helluva offense. But I remember running into some of Houston's players at the airport on the way back home. They called us every name in the book, because they thought we had dogged it by playing for the tie.

I remember beating Florida in the rain down in Jacksonville in 1968. I thought it was going to be a tough game, but Cavan was throwing the ball all over the place, and they couldn't stop us. We won big—51–0—and a week later we went to Auburn and won 17–3 to clinch another championship. After all those years of watching Vanderbilt struggle, Georgia had won two SEC championships in my first three seasons. I didn't know how long that run was going to last, but I was enjoying myself!

The only other strong memory I have of those first few years is when we went out to the Sun Bowl in El Paso to play Nebraska (in 1969). The wind was blowing 45 miles an hour, and it looked like they had the wind at their backs all day. Man, they just beat our socks off, 45–6.

Before long I had developed a pretty good relationship with Vince Dooley. Tuesday was the only day that I could go over there. I would show up for practice, and Dooley would stop whatever he was doing and start walking around the field with me. He would tell me anything that I asked. And if there was some injury or something bugging him, he would discuss that too. After practice we would go to his house and have dinner. Barbara and all of the kids were there, and we would surround this big table. Kids were doing what kids do, and Vince would read the newspaper. I really enjoyed those evenings, and I appreciated Vince and Barbara having me over.

I would show up for practice, and Dooley would stop whatever he was doing and start walking around the field with me.

I remember one afternoon Erk Russell called me and asked me to meet him in his office. He told me that he had broken down the offense of the team that we were going to play that Saturday, and he asked if I would like to look at what he had. So he walked me into one of those film rooms and showed me everything he had done. He had taken the opponent's whole offense from the week before and broken it down. From that point on he and I started talking every Friday. No coach had ever done that. Erk was a helluva motivator of football players, probably the best I've ever seen. He once told me why he never had a whole lot of size on the defensive line. He said that every spring Dooley would pluck out all of his big defensive linemen and move them over to the offense. Dooley took all his size. I don't know if that is true or not, but it makes for a great story. Erk was just one helluva guy. I can't believe he's gone.

I'm not sure exactly what I expected when I got to Georgia, but I sure was surprised to win two championships in the first three years.

I'm not sure exactly what I expected when I got to Georgia, but I sure was surprised to win two championships in the first three years. But the world was getting ready to change in the 1970s, and we had to get ready to change with it.

CHAPTER 9

The '70s:
From Appleby to
Washington to
Wonder Dogs

The radio crew in the late 1970s. Left to right: spotter Louis Phillips, me, spotter Dick Payne, color man Phil Schaefer. Behind them is engineer Hugh Christian. PHOTO COURTESY OF THE UNIVERSITY OF GEORGIA

I do remember screaming,
"My God, Georgia has beaten
Tennessee in Knoxville."
People told me that was the first
time I had really let myself go.
That was news to me, because I
thought I had always let myself go.
I had never given that a thought.

Everybody knows how tough the late '60s were in our country. There was change coming, and it was coming big in college football and basketball in the South.

If you worked in the South you knew the time had come to recruit the black athlete. They had been shut out for so long in the SEC. I remember when Vanderbilt was getting ready to sign its first African American basketball player, Perry Wallace. We were at the NCAA tournament in Lexington, Kentucky, in 1965, and getting ready to play Michigan for a spot in the Final Four. I put him on our radio broadcast, because by then it was clear that he was coming to Vanderbilt. But some people objected to it. I never understood why. It was the right thing to do.

Perry was a great, great kid. He went to school in Nashville at Pearl High, where he was the valedictorian of his senior class. He could flat-out jump. We signed him at Vanderbilt, and he became the first African American athlete to complete four years at an SEC school.

After Bear Bryant at Alabama got beat by Southern Cal in 1970 he started signing African American players. Then the other schools in the conference followed suit. At Georgia we immediately got some great players such as Horace King, a super running back.

One thing was for sure. When it came to college football, the '70s were going to be a lot different from the '60s.

One thing was for sure. When it came to college football, the '70s were going to be a lot different from the '60s. I have so many great memories from that decade.

I can remember Buzy Rosenberg returning a couple of punts for touchdowns against Oregon State in 1971. Man, he could run all over the field. We've had some great punt returners, but I would put him up there with Jake Scott and Scott Woerner as the best we've had.

That '71 team was a very good team. We had struggled the year before and ended up with a 5–5 record, but the '71 team had a bunch of really good young players. Andy Johnson was a sophomore and a great, great quarterback. He knew how to run the veer offense.

How can anyone ever forget the 1971 game we had with Auburn? Both of us were undefeated and thinking we were good enough to win the SEC championship. Pat Sullivan was in the Heisman Trophy race, and he was throwing the ball all over the place. We would hit him, and he would throw it falling down and still complete it. And he had the little receiver Terry Beasley who could get open and catch everything. They had a little too much for us that day, and we lost a tough one. (Note: On November 13, 1971, Sullivan completed 14 of 24 passes for 248 yards and four touchdowns as Auburn defeated Georgia 35–20 in Athens. Based on his performance against the Bulldogs, Sullivan won the 1971 Heisman Trophy.)

A couple of weeks later, on Thanksgiving night, we played Georgia Tech at Grant Field. Earlier in the day Nebraska and Oklahoma played one of the greatest college football games ever. (Note: On November 25, 1971, No. 1 Nebraska beat No. 2 Oklahoma 35–31 in what became known as "the Game of the Century.")

But at the same time the Nebraska-Oklahoma game was going on, the Tech and Georgia freshmen were playing their annual game. A bunch of the media guys who came to watch the freshman game brought little portable TVs so that they could keep up with Nebraska-Oklahoma. But the Tech athletic director, Bobby Dodd, didn't like that, and so everybody had to check their TVs until after the freshman game. Man, did the media get mad about that!

It was a great game, and we trailed all night long. But then Andy Johnson drove us down the field. The tight end, Mike Greene, made a big catch to keep the drive alive, and Jimmy Poulos went over the top. It seemed to be dark as the devil when we scored, but it was a great ballgame. (Note: Poulos leaped over the Georgia Tech defense for a touchdown with only 14 seconds left as Georgia rallied to beat Georgia Tech 28–24.)

A lot of people have told me over the years that our 1973 game at Tennessee was big in terms of my relationship with the Georgia people. I think that's true, because a lot of Georgia people told me that later on. We were behind 31–21 and had no shot at winning, I thought. But then we scored two touchdowns late and won the thing when Andy Johnson scored. I do remember screaming, "My God, Georgia has beaten Tennessee in Knoxville!" People told me that was the first time I had really let myself go. That was news to me, because I thought I had always let myself go. I had never given that a thought. I guess winning at Tennessee meant so much to me because I had been there so many times with Vanderbilt and left disappointed.

We had a helluva year in 1975. The year before we weren't very good on defense, and that just killed Erk. So he came up with the idea of calling his defense the Junkyard Dawgs because they were a mean, scrappy bunch of guys who were not very big. That turned out to be a pretty good group, and they bailed our fannies out of more than one game.

I remember that we opened the season against Tony Dorsett and Pittsburgh. Man, they were good. Johnny Majors had gone there as head coach and signed something like 120 guys his first year and was building a helluva team. They beat us 19–9 in Athens. I remember hearing from the guys on the field that they were calling our players a bunch of names, trying to get something started. The next year we would have to play them again in the Sugar Bowl, and they beat us to win the national championship. Pittsburgh was really something.

I remember hearing from the guys on the field that they were calling our players a bunch of names, trying to get something started.

The defense really saved us in 1975 when we went down to Jacksonville to play Florida. We couldn't move the ball against their defense. They were moving up and down the field on us, but just about all the yardage was between the 20s. We kept stopping them and just sort of kept hanging around. Finally, we pulled out a trick play that we had been working on all week. Richard Appleby had been running the reverse all season and I think had run it once or twice that day. We were still behind, 7–3, when he took the ball and didn't run it. He threw it to Gene Washington, who had gotten behind the Florida defense. We won 10–7, and everybody went nuts. What a great day. I didn't tell anybody until after the game, but I had gotten tipped off that the trick play was coming.

Bill Pace put in the veer offense when he got there as our offensive coordinator in 1974, and no team ever ran it better than the 1976 team. We had a huge offensive line that was really good. Ray Goff was the best quarterback we ever had at running the option. We had some great running backs. That was just a very good team, and they proved it by winning the SEC championship.

A couple of games really stick out from that year. I remember the guys shaving their heads before the season started, and that was a really big deal. We opened the season against California, and they had a great quarterback, Joe Roth, who just threw the ball all over the place. We didn't know it at the time, but the kid had cancer. (Note: Georgia defeated California 36–24 in the 1976 season-opener. California quarterback Joe Roth played the entire season with cancer. He died on February 19, 1977.)

We played Alabama in Athens on October 2, 1976, and Bear Bryant was in the middle of his incredible run (Note: From 1971 to 1981 Bryant and Alabama won 116 games, nine SEC championships, and three national championships.) Our people had been talking about that game all summer, and it was just a wild, wild day in Athens. We beat them up pretty good, 21–0, because our defense just absolutely shut them down. What I remember most was the traffic. I'm not sure anybody went home after that game.

We went back down to Jacksonville, and after the 1975 game with Florida we didn't know what to expect. We knew they were pretty mad. In the first half they handled us pretty good. But their coach, Doug Dickey, faked a punt when they were still ahead. After that we just crushed them. I remember Goff was really good in that game. (Note: After Georgia trailed 27–13, senior quarterback Ray Goff scored three touchdowns and rallied the Bulldogs to a 41–27 victory.)

During the 1978 season we kept winning one close game after another. They called us the "Wonder Dogs" because we just kept finding ways to win. (Note: The 1978 Georgia team posted four of its nine wins by a total of six points. In that season Georgia had five games decided by three points or less.)

I remember that we were down 17–7 at halftime at LSU, and it looked like we were in trouble. But then Lindsay Scott returned the second-half kickoff 99 yards for a touchdown, and suddenly we were back in it. After that we were in control and found a way to get out of there with a 24–17 win.

People still talk about the 1978 Kentucky game when we were on the road and just got stuck in a huge hole up there. (Note: On

October 28, 1978, Georgia trailed 16–0 at Kentucky before starting its comeback.) We finally got the ball back late, trailing by a couple of points, 16–14. We just drove down the field behind Jeff Pyburn, our quarterback, and running back Willie McClendon, who was just running all over people late in the game. We finally got Rex Robinson into position to kick the winning field goal. At that point things were crazy, and when he kicked it through, I never said it was good. I just screamed, "Yeah! Yeah! Yeah! Yeah!" I thought later that maybe I should have said something else, but it was emotional. We had been doing stuff like that all year.

We missed out on our shot to win the conference title (Note: Alabama won the SEC championship with a 6–0 record, and Georgia finished second at 5–0–1) when we had a 22–22 tie with Auburn that just absolutely destroyed us. We had found a way to win those kinds of games all year, but we could not win that one.

But then we turned around and played one of the damndest games you could ever hope to see, against Georgia Tech. I heard Dooley say one time that the game had everything, and he was right. We fell behind 20–0 and then came back and took the lead when Scott Woerner returned a punt about 100 miles. (Note: Woerner returned a punt 72 yards for a touchdown to give Georgia a 21–20 lead.) Then their guy, Drew Hill, went 101 yards on the next kickoff, and then they were back on top. We had put Buck Belue in the game because we needed something to shake up the offense. And it worked. It was fourth down, and Buck threw to Amp Arnold, who had gotten behind the Tech defense, for a touchdown.

But then we turned around and played one of the damndest games you could ever hope to see, against Georgia Tech.

Dooley decided to go for two and the win. He didn't hesitate. Buck's pass was incomplete, but our guy, tight end Mark Hodge, had gotten knocked down, and a bunch of flags came out for interference. Then Buck pitched to Amp for the two points, and we won 29–28.

Dooley decided to go for two and the win. He didn't hesitate.

Man, that was a crazy year.

The 1979 season wasn't a whole lot of fun, because we lost to all of those ACC teams. (Note: In 1979 Georgia lost 22–21 to Wake Forest; 12–7 to Clemson; 27–20 to former ACC member South Carolina; and 31–0 to Virginia, on Homecoming. Georgia finished 6–5 and did not go to a bowl game.)

So the 1970s were okay. We won one championship in 1976, but we came really close another time or two.

When the decade ended, we had no idea what the '80s would bring. We didn't know that a kid out of Johnson County was coming to shake things up. Man, was he going to shake things up.

CHAPTER 10
The '80s:
There Goes Herschel!
There Goes Herschel!

We had no idea that Herschel Walker would be as good as he was until an unforgettable night in Knoxville, Tennessee. I don't think we'll ever see another one like Herschel. PHOTO COURTESY OF AP IMAGES

*When you go back and look
at the film you can see the
South Carolina players coming
over to make the tackle.
They took what they thought was
the right angle, but when they got
to the spot, Herschel was gone.
He was just so fast.*

We really had no reason to think that 1980 was going to be anything special. A lot of those freshmen and sophomores from that good 1978 team were now juniors and seniors. So that gave us a chance, I guess.

We had no idea that we were about to have the greatest season in Georgia football history with the guy who may go down as the greatest player we've ever had

When we signed Herschel Walker earlier in the year it was a pretty big story because we had to fight tooth and nail with Clemson to get him. I don't think Clemson ever got over the fact that we got him and they didn't. But once he got into camp, I never heard back that he was doing anything remarkable or out of the ordinary. I just figured that he was another kid who was going to have to learn the ropes.

I've told this story before, but Dooley told me that he was concerned that he might have a big, stiff fullback on this hands. That is what he said to me. But once we got to Knoxville for the opener on September 6, we knew differently. It didn't take us long to figure out that we had something pretty damn special.

We were getting beat pretty good—15–2—by Tennessee when Herschel scored his first touchdown by running over Bill Bates. I mean, Bates went on to have a pretty good pro career with the Cowboys, and he had time to get ready to make the tackle in the right manner. But rHerschel just got his pads up under Bates *But Herschel just got his pads up under Bates and just plowed right through him.* and just plowed right through him. Then later in the game Herschel scored on a sweep to the left to give us the lead, and we held on by the skin of our teeth to win 16–15.

Yeah, I guess you could say that I got pretty excited that night. I remember yelling, "My God Almighty, he ran right through two men!" Later on, when I heard the tape, I knew I had said "My God, a freshman!"

I didn't think anything about it at the time, because to me that was just part of the ballgame. I just blurted out what I felt at the time. But man, did I hear from the church crowd! Elmo Ellis of WSB called me to let me know that some people had called the radio station and were complaining. He wanted me to sort of answer it because some people were upset about it. I really didn't understand that.

I do remember that after the Tennessee game a bunch of us were talking about the schedule and looking ahead to what might happen. Herschel was just so big and so strong. But I remember that in the Tennessee game we saw his strength, but we didn't really see his great foot speed. We would see that that next week against Texas A&M. He broke off a big one and just ran away for 75 yards. That was really something to see. That was when I really knew that if we could get a few breaks, we had a chance to be pretty good. And we were good. I have many fond memories of that season.

I just blurted out what I felt at the time. But man, did I hear from the church crowd!

We beat Clemson 20–16 at home because of Scott Woerner. He had a 67-yard punt return for a score and a 98-yard interception return to set up another score. He was incredible that day. Clemson had a bunch of yards and we hardly had any, but we somehow won the game. That was the first of a bunch of great games we would have with Clemson over the next six or seven years. The fans of both schools would go back and forth with each other about recruiting wars and the rumors of recruiting wars. Each side questioned how the other side got their players. And the games were just bloodbaths. God, that was a great series.

People always ask me about my favorite run that Herschel made that season. I can't say that I had a favorite, but I can tell you one that impressed me. Herschel had his big 76-yard run for a score against South Carolina. There was a hole at the right tackle, and when he popped through it he was gone down the South Carolina sideline. When you go back and look at the film you can see the South Carolina players coming over to make the tackle. They took what they thought was the right angle, but when they got to the spot, Herschel was gone. He was just so fast.

That game was when Herschel went head-to-head with George Rogers, the great South Carolina running back. They were both up for the Heisman Trophy. In the pregame or halftime show, I don't remember which one it was, Loran Smith lined me up to talk to Dick Young, the famous sportswriter from the *New York Daily News*. Loran wanted me to pin Young down on who he was going to vote for in the Heisman Trophy race. So I just asked the guy right out. "I'm not voting for a freshman," he said.

Rogers had a big fumble that day at the end of the game, which helped us win. He was a great player, but I thought Herschel out-played him that day. I know a freshman has never won the Heisman Trophy, but Herschel was good enough that year to win it.

Herschel was a polite, well-liked kid. There was really no one else like him before or since. We had a coach in Dooley who really liked to run the football. And we had a guy in Herschel who ran it like nobody I've ever seen. Maybe Bo Jackson could be put in that conversation. A bunch of us used to talk all the time about Herschel and Bo and which one was the best. I think if you put them in track suits and just let them run flat-out, Herschel nips him. But Bo was such an incredible athlete who could do everything. If he didn't get hurt, and if Auburn had used him the right way during his career, Bo could have put up some staggering numbers.

When we got down to Jacksonville to play Florida we had an undefeated 8–0 record and were ranked No. 2. Notre Dame was No. 1

and was playing at Georgia Tech that day. But to tell you the truth we weren't paying attention to that game, because we had our hands pretty damn full down in Jacksonville.

Herschel was a polite, well-liked kid. There was really no one else like him before or since.

Everybody remembers Buck's pass to Lindsay Scott for the winning touchdown, but there was a lot of stuff going on that day before that great moment. I remember that they put the Florida coaches in the booth right next to us at the old Gator Bowl. Apparently they didn't have an electrical outlet in that wooden booth, and one young coach really got upset with that. So he tried to reach around into our booth and plug one of his things in. My spotter, Louis Phillips, always had a little chip on his shoulder. He didn't want to help the guy, but he did.

So after the game ended as suddenly as it did, that same young coach was mad and trying to pull his plug out of the socket that was in our booth. Louis stopped him from doing it and told him to relax. Well, the young coach didn't relax. The place was still in an uproar. So Louis and this young coach were getting into it, and I thought they were going to fight out in the hall. But they settled down, and no punches were thrown. That would have been a mess.

One of the other great memories of that game was looking down on the field after the big play from Belue to Scott. At one end there were all of these people just all over Lindsay. But in the middle of the field, lying on the ground, Buck was just holding his hands on his headgear like he was laughing. One guy was kneeling over him.

I don't remember when we got word that Tech had tied Notre Dame 3–3 back in Atlanta. But after the game we knew that we were going to be No. 1, so we had our shot.

We clinched the championship at Auburn 31–21 and then took care of Georgia Tech 38–20 to finish undefeated. We were going to play Notre Dame in the Sugar Bowl for everything.

I resented not being able to go to that bowl game. But Texaco was still doing the games, so I couldn't call it. So my spotter Dick Payne and I took our wives to Athens and treated it just like a football weekend. We checked into the old Down Towner Motel and settled in to watch the game. I don't think our wives were particularly excited about that.

The thing that I remember about that game is Notre Dame letting that kickoff go and our guy, Bob Kelly,

We clinched the championship at Auburn 31–21 and then took care of Georgia Tech 38–20 to finish undefeated.

jumping on it near their goal line. We found a way to win that game, 17–10, just like we had won all the rest. We had come so close before. Man, that looked like a helluva celebration in New Orleans.

The next three years, 1981 to 1983, were really something. (Note: From 1980 to 1983 Georgia had its greatest four-year run in its history as the Bulldogs went 43–4–1 with three SEC championships and one national championship.) A couple of memories from 1981 really stick out. We went up to Clemson and just kept laying the ball on the ground. Their rush just came right up the middle, and at times Buck Belue just didn't have a chance. They beat us 13–3. (Note: After that win over Georgia, Clemson finished the season undefeated and beat Nebraska in the Orange Bowl for the national championship.)

The other memory I have came from the Sugar Bowl against Pittsburgh. They had Dan Marino, and he had a cannon for an arm. I think earlier in the week before the game we had lost one of our defensive backs that we used in passing situations. It looked like we had them beat, but they had a fourth down late. We blitzed Marino, and he just found John Brown right down the middle for a touchdown. (Note: With only 35 seconds left, Marino hit Brown for a 33-yard touchdown pass to give Pittsburgh a 24–20 win over Georgia. The Bulldogs finished the season 10–2.)

Here are a few more memories from the 1980s:

- In 1982 I knew we were going to have a tough time at Auburn. It was always a tough place for us to finish, especially when there was a championship on the line. But we got a 19–14 lead late, and then our defense had to hold on for dear life. There are two things that I'm always going to remember about Auburn's final drive. One is Dale Carver coming off the corner to get a big sack and put them in a deep hole. The other is the final play, a pass that got broken up in our end zone. On that play, I found out later on, Bo Jackson was wide open out in the flat. But the Auburn quarterback, Randy Campbell, didn't see him. Bo was wide open, and if he had caught the ball he would have run for a million miles. In fact, somebody sent me a picture of that final play, and you can see that Bo is wide open. Bo was just a freshman that year, and Auburn had a lot of really good backs, but I don't think they used Bo the right way.

  That was the game when I asked our guys on defense to "hunker down" during Auburn's final drive and ended it with, "Look at the sugar falling out of the sky." It was a great deal.

- No one had a hint, at least I didn't hear a hint, that Herschel was going to leave us early. It just happened so quick, and all of a sudden it was over. He was gone, and it was an incredible shock. For a long time I wondered what would have happened if Herschel had come back for the 1983 season. Would we have won another championship? Instead we lost at the end of the year to Auburn, 13–7, and by then they had figured out how to use Bo. That game was in Athens. What if Herschel had been there? How huge would that have been?

♦ We didn't win the championship in 1983, but we had a pretty good finish at 9–1–1, and we played Texas in the Cotton Bowl. Texas was ranked No. 2, and if they had beaten us they would have had a shot at the national championship. Man, they were a lot better than us. But we got a break when they fumbled a punt and we got it. John Lastinger ran for the touchdown, and we beat those guys 10–9. Texas had one of the best defenses I've ever seen, and we beat those guys!

♦ I have a picture on the wall of my dining room of Kevin Butler making the 60-yard field goal to beat Clemson 26–23 in 1984. He signed it for me. When you look at it you can see Kevin's eyes looking at the ball after he kicked it. I've often wondered if he knew how far he had kicked it. Did he know It was going to be good when it left his foot?

♦ In 1984 we went to Birmingham and beat Alabama 24–14. Pulpwood Smith had a couple of early runs up the middle for touchdowns. I remember that he said that he was going to make people forget about Herschel. That game turned out to be about the best one he ever had.

♦ We finished 1984 in the Citrus Bowl against Florida State. They had a big reputation for blocking punts. We were leading the game 17–9 and were about to win when they blocked a punt and scored. We ended up tying those guys 17–17. They sent Butler out there to kick a long one on the last play of the game, and it came up short.

I have so many more memories from the 1980s. There was the time in 1985 when we beat Florida when they were No. 1. That was a stunner. Or the time we went to Auburn in 1986 and they turned the water on us after we beat them. The guy spraying that water turned it up into the first 25 rows or so in the stands, and that got a lot of people upset. Then we came to find out that the guy giving the orders at Auburn was a Georgia grad, Kermit Perry. That was a crazy night.

But the thing that I didn't see coming in the late '80s was Dooley deciding to retire in December 1988. I had no indication that he was going to do that. Our regular Tuesday meetings had wound down because I was working for WSB in the afternoons. But as soon as Vince announced that he was stepping down, the speculation started going fast and furious over who was going to be the new coach.

But the thing that I didn't see coming in the late '80s was Dooley deciding to retire in December 1988.

It looked like it was going to be Dick Sheridan, the coach at N.C. State. The search committee met with him out at the Holiday Inn on I-85 near Commerce. I thought that deal was done, but for whatever reason it didn't work out.

I thought Erk Russell was going to get the job. He had been with us a long time—17 years—before he went to Georgia Southern to build that program. And from what I heard Erk felt he was definitely up for the job. He was out in Idaho with his Georgia Southern team when all of this was going on. But I later heard that Erk cooled on the idea of the job and decided not to take it. Then people came out and said that Erk was never offered the job. I don't know if that was the truth, but I do know that was not a good thing.

Then everybody went down to Jacksonville for Vince's last game against Michigan State at the Gator Bowl. What I remember most about the game was that Dooley let offensive coordinator George Haffner call the entire game, and Haffner decided to turn Wayne Johnson, our quarterback, loose. We were going pretty good, but we never could pull away, because every time we tried, Michigan State's Andre Rison would make some kind of incredible play to keep them in it. We ended up winning 34–27, but it sure wasn't easy.

After the game the story started to leak out that Ray Goff was going to be the next coach. I remember that some people liked the idea, but other people weren't so fond of it. Then there was the press conference at the hotel, introducing Ray as the next head coach. It was a strange feeling at that press conference, looking at Dooley and knowing that he was done.

All I knew is that I had been at Georgia for 22 years, and Dooley was the only coach I'd ever known. The world was about to change, and nobody quite knew what to expect.

> *It was a strange feeling at that press conference, looking at Dooley and knowing that he was done.*

ATLANTA FALCONS

Brad Nessler left the Falcons radio team in 1988, so I got a chance to work with the Atlanta Falcons for several seasons, from 1988 to 1991.

I thought it would be a good thing to do. I had seen other guys work college football on Saturdays and pro football on Sundays. They talked a lot about the travel, and I was a little concerned about that because Georgia played a lot of night games.

But I was lucky. My engineer, Rick Shaw, was also working the Georgia games on Saturday, so I could travel with him. Rick had been everywhere and seen everything, and he knew every ticket agent in the world. So that helped a lot.

The guys I knew who were doing both college and pro ball had not worked in the Southeastern Conference. Getting from Starkville to San Francisco is no easy deal, let me tell you that. I remember they put us on this extremely small plane, and there just wasn't enough room for everybody. I didn't know if the damn thing was going to get off the ground. One of the guys who showed up to ride with us was inebriated and got stuck in the toilet and broke the mirror in the bathroom. It was a helluva ride.

We get to San Francisco about 5:00 in the morning, and then everybody on the crew is supposed to have breakfast together at 7:00 AM. Welcome to the NFL.

But I do remember those breakfasts on Sunday mornings on the road. Mike Kenn and our offensive line would always come down to join us. And then they must have had some kind of cue, because the entire offensive line would get up and leave for the stadium. So I'd just get up and fall in right behind them because I had to tape some stuff in the locker room for the pregame show.

They would sit around the locker room, read the Sunday sports pages, and just give a guy hell if his college team had lost the day before. I would just sit there and listen to all of it. It was a great thing to be a part of.

I remember when we got Deion Sanders and the first game he played for us. We had paid a ton of money for him, and in the first game he took a punt like 70 yards for a touchdown. (Note: On Sunday, September 10, 1989, Deion Sanders returned a punt 68 yards for a touchdown against the Los Angeles Rams in his first NFL game.) I remember that I went pretty nuts and looked over at team owner Rankin Smith. His face was flushed because he was pretty excited.

My partner in the booth was Jeff Van Note, a former great Falcons player and a real hoot. Van Note was a newspaper fanatic. Every Sunday morning he would get up to go run and would come back with every Sunday paper that he could find. The man read everything he could get his hands on. Then on Sunday night he would get on the plane and could barely get down the aisle because he had so much stuff. He was doing Kentucky football on Saturdays. Van Note is a special guy, and he is still a great friend.

We had two young, big-armed quarterbacks named Brett Favre and Billy Joe Tolliver. They got to arguing one day on a flight to L.A. about who had the strongest arm. So when we got there the team went out to the stadium for a walk through. Favre and Tolliver were still arguing. So they got dressed and went out to the 50-yard line. They started throwing balls and trying to see how many they could throw over the roof at the other end. The rest of the Falcons players were hanging back taking bets on who was going to win. I don't remember who eventually won, but it was a helluva thing to watch because those guys could really sling it. Of course Favre left us and went on to be great with the Packers.

It's funny the things you remember. I remember that before each home game at the old Atlanta-Fulton County Stadium a big shipment of doughnuts would come to the ticket office. I would be at the stadium so early that I would go down and get doughnuts for Rick Shaw and Skinny Bobby Harper, who was helping us on the broadcast. Then I would light a cigar and go for a long walk around the stadium. That would become my ritual.

I remember that on home games I would leave my house in Marietta and stop at the same McDonalds. I would take only the sports section into the place with me and get a sausage biscuit.

I only did the Falcons for a short time, and a big reason why was the coach, Jerry Glanville. I thought Glanville was a capable coach, but he went about it in an odd way. I remember being in the airport one day, and then out of the blue Glanville came up and shouted at me, "Munson, you've got to get excited!"

I asked him what the hell he was talking about.

Then he said it again: "You've got to get excited!"

I really had no idea what he was talking about. I always thought that if I had a fault as a broadcaster it was that sometimes I would get too excited.

Ultimately Glanville told the Falcons brass he wanted his own announcer, and he told them that he "didn't want all that Georgia bullshit!" It bothered me that someone with Glanville's loud personality was allowed to make that kind of decision. I missed it immediately. I thought the two jobs were tied together and I would retire working the double football thing. But he wanted his own guy, and he got me out.

But I will never forget Deion taking that punt return all the way and how he just electrified that stadium. And I will never forget those doughnuts. Those were some damned good doughnuts.

CHAPTER II

The '90s: Close but No Cigar

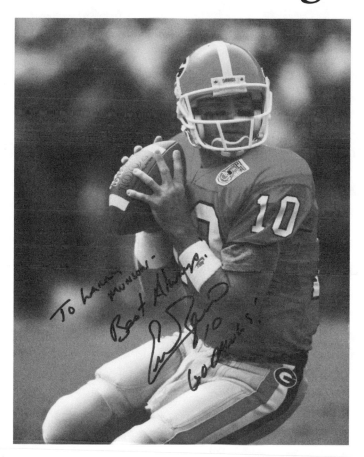

In the 1990s Eric Zeier changed the way we played offense at Georgia. He could really throw it. He later came to work for our radio crew.

In 1992 I thought we had a helluva football team. Zeier was our quarterback. Garrison Hearst was our running back, and he was going to have a great year. But we lost two games that just broke our hearts.

The 1990s didn't get off to a particularly good start for me. Georgia was really struggling and went 4–7 in the 1990 season. Back then I was also doing the Falcons. We were out in San Francisco, and I was getting ready to get off the charter plane and walk down a flight of steps. All of a sudden my legs buckled, and I fell down that entire flight of steps. They picked me up, and the next thing I heard was that I was going to need back surgery. The Clemson game that season—a 34–3 loss on October 6—was the first Georgia game I had ever missed.

Ray's teams struggled for a couple of years, but recruiting started to pick up, and we signed Eric Zeier as our quarterback. That kid could throw. Then we hired Wayne McDuffie as our offensive coordinator, and it became clear that things were getting ready to change.

There were a lot of interesting guys on Goff's staff. But none was more interesting than Wayne McDuffie. He was such a quiet guy but very, very smart. When we were on the road for games, some of the radio crew and I would get up on Saturday morning and go for a walk. We would walk long distances, and every time we did it we would see McDuffie out there running. Sometimes when we would see McDuffie we would try to walk along with him and talk. But he would keep going. He was very much a quiet loner. He was a very good football coach, and I hate the way it ended for him. (Note: On February 16, 1996, Wayne McDuffie, who had two tours of duty as an assistant coach at Georgia, died of a self-inflicted gunshot wound.)

Sometimes when we would see McDuffie we would try to walk along with him and talk. But he would keep going.

I thought Ray really had good football knowledge, but sometimes it seemed like he thought everyone was against him. He felt that WSB was not handling the phone calls right on the Sunday night show. There were people from Athens who would call in, and they would be very rough. He thought we should block them off better.

He tried hard and thought that if he had gotten a little more cooperation he could have made it. He was a damned good recruiter.

Ray was always good to me. He had been a great quarterback for us, and he worked very, very hard once he got the job. He knew that I really liked one particular power-sweep play that we would run. It was the old Southern Cal sweep. Some people called it the "Packers sweep." So whenever he ran it Ray would always ask me later, "Did you see your play?" I appreciated that.

While it didn't end well for Ray, the team had some great moments when he was there. We had that Clemson game in 1991 when the crowd was really wild. Zeier threw a 59-yard bomb to Arthur Marshall, and that set up a score right before halftime. Clemson was ranked No. 6, and nobody gave us a shot. But we beat those guys. I remember that the crowd was also buzzing because the Braves had won the division earlier in the day. That was quite a night. (Note: On October 5, 1991, freshman quarterback Eric Zeier threw for 249 yards and two touchdowns as Georgia upset No. 6 Clemson 27–12. Earlier in the day the Atlanta Braves clinched the first of what would become 14 straight division titles.)

So whenever he ran it Ray would always ask me later, "Did you see your play?"

In 1992 I thought we had a helluva football team. Zeier was our quarterback. Garrison Hearst was our running back, and he was going to have a great year. But we lost two games that just broke our hearts.

We lost 34–31 to Tennessee at home when it seemed like we turned the ball over a million times. (Note: Georgia had six turnovers in the game—four fumbles and two interceptions.) Their quarterback scored late, and they beat us. (Note: Tennessee's Heath Shuler, who would later become a congressman from the 11th district of his native

North Carolina, scored the winning touchdown against Georgia with only 50 seconds left.)

The thing I remember about losing 26–24 to Florida in Jacksonville is that we were moving the ball against them. Georgia had a bunch (408 yards) of total offense, and all we had to do was get the ball back one more time, and we had a shot to beat them. But their quarterback, Shane Matthews, made a big throw late, and they were able to hold on to the ball. (Note: Matthews converted a crucial third-and-13 with a pass to Harrison Houston. That gave Florida an important first down, and the Gators held on for the win.) Man, that was a killer.

The football gods gave one back to us when we played Auburn two weeks later. We were leading 14–10, but Auburn was getting ready to score in the final seconds. They were on about the 1-yard line, and they decided to run the ball. It came loose, and our guys just kind of piled in there. People were jumping around, and I looked up at the clock, and the time was running out. They never got another play off, and we won. I think I said that "we saved ourselves" because that is exactly what happened.

We had a bunch of close losses when Ray was there. We had a heartbreaker at Alabama when we lost on a late field goal. (Note: Georgia held a 28–19 lead at Alabama in 1994 going into the fourth quarter. But Alabama rallied and Michael Proctor kicked a 32-yard field goal with 1:12 left to beat Georgia 29–28.) What I remember most about that game is the trip out of Tuscaloosa. Neil "Hondo" Williamson was driving, and we fell in behind the team buses with the police escort. We *I kept telling Hondo he was going to turn the car over.* get on the shoulder of the road and passed a million cars. I kept telling Hondo he was going to turn the car over. But we got out of there.

But that 1992 team, which was 10–2, was really Ray's shot at a championship. We struggled after that, and eventually they let him go after the 1995 season. (Note: Goff's final three seasons at Georgia, he posted records of 5–6, 6–4–1, and 6–6.)

It took Ray a while to warm up to us on the radio side, but at the end, after he was let go, he took the whole crowd out to pizza one night. He didn't realize how many friends he had in the radio business. He was a good man, but he was sensitive.

But Jim Donnan was even more sensitive. I'm not sure why, but nobody seemed to get along with Donnan when he first got to Georgia in December 1995. First of all, he had gotten the job under very unusual circumstances.

Glen Mason was at Kansas and had done a good job there. Dooley hired him at Georgia, and he came and had a press conference in Athens. He was the guy. But it seemed like during the press conference (on December 18, 1995), he was already starting to have second thoughts. Then all of a sudden he changed his mind, and we were looking for another coach. (Note: On Christmas Day 1995, just one week after he had accepted the job at Georgia, Glen Mason announced that he had changed his mind and would remain at Kansas. Before the end of the day, Georgia athletics director Vince Dooley had hired Jim Donnan, the head coach at Marshall.)

Donnan wanted me to be at every practice. He thought that I should be there learning his system. He didn't understand that I was really on his side, and it took him a while to realize that. It seemed that he had a chip on his shoulder all the time. We never had an outbreak of words or anything like that, but it did get back to me that he had made remarks to people that "Munson needs to get with the program."

But the fact is that Donnan was doing a much better job than he got credit for. He and his staff were bringing in some studs as players. And people didn't appreciate what Donnan did until after he was gone. Man, we had some wild games when he was here.

We had that four-overtime thing at Auburn in 1996, when we scored on the last play of the game. Then it seemed like we were out there nine years before we finally won. (Note: On November 16, 1996, at Auburn, Mike Bobo threw a 30-yard touchdown pass to Corey Allen on the last play of regulation to tie the game at 28–28. Georgia eventually won 56–49 in what was the first overtime game in SEC history.)

Why does it seem that all of the crazy things happen at Auburn? The guy threw the drink on us there in 1982. They turned the water hoses on our fans after we beat them in 1986. I guess it was 1994 when we came from behind and tied them. (Note: On November 12, 1994, Georgia trailed Auburn 23–9 in the third quarter. Georgia rallied to tie the Tigers

Why does it seem that all of the crazy things happen at Auburn?

23–23. Until then Auburn had won 20 straight games under second-year coach Terry Bowden.) That was a helluva game, but what I remember was parking before the game. There is this big lot out near the main road, and a bunch of Georgia people park out there so they can get a head start getting out of town. Hondo was riding with me, and we pulled into that lot. I may have moved a chair or something to get us a space, because there was plenty of room. But there was this woman, and she was madder than hell! Somebody told her it was me, and she screamed, "I don't give a good goddamn who he is! I was here first!" Man, she was hot. I was totally convinced that the car was going to be destroyed when we got back, but it wasn't.

I remember the game in 1997 when we finally beat Florida. We had been getting killed by those guys since Steve Spurrier came to Florida in 1990. There were a lot of people, and I was probably one of them, who wondered if we were ever going to beat those guys again. I remember that in the airport somebody gave me a cigar and told me to light it after we beat Florida. Our game producer, Larry

England, took the cigar from me and said he was going to keep it until I was ready for it. In the second half we were in control of the game, and Larry pulled out the cigar and even lit it for me. Larry England was a very good man. I remember feeling pretty good about that game when it was over. (Note: On November 1, 1997, Georgia defeated Florida 37–17 in Jacksonville. Florida coach Steve Spurrier had beaten Georgia seven straight seasons before the win.)

Our game producer, Larry England, took the cigar from me and said he was going to keep it until I was ready for it.

Then we had those three wild games in a row with Georgia Tech in 1997 through 1999. The first one, a 27–24 win in 1997, was the one where it looked like we had no shot. But Bobo hit Allen down in the corner, and Allen got like half of his foot in bounds. (Note: On November 29, 1997, in Atlanta, Georgia trailed Georgia Tech 24–21 with 48 seconds left. Bobo drove Georgia 65 yards and hit Allen with an eight-yard touchdown pass with eight seconds left to give Georgia the victory.)

But after that win Donnan lost three straight to Tech, including that crazy 51–48 loss in Atlanta (on November 27, 1999). I can still see Jasper Sanks hitting the ground and that ball coming loose and those officials calling it a fumble when it wasn't.

Then the next year, in 2000, we lost to Tech again, 27–15, and they beat us up pretty good. That's what did Donnan in.

I see Donnan out having dinner sometimes in Athens, and we will speak for a moment. Sometimes I wonder how things would have worked out if he had stayed, because he really got us some good players.

But there we were, heading into a new century and wondering if we were ever going to win another championship. I had been fortunate to be a part of six SEC championships in my first 17 years at

In 1966, my first year at Georgia, we won the SEC championship. Who knew it was going to happen that quickly? It was the first of eight conference championship teams I had the privilege of covering.

Coach Dooley and me on the practice fields, sometime in the 1970s. I used to drive him crazy before games. PHOTO COURTESY OF THE UNIVERSITY OF GEORGIA

Rex Robinson made the field goal to beat Kentucky in 1978. That's when I just screamed, "Yeah! Yeah! Yeah! Yeah!"

Buck Belue almost played professional baseball instead of coming to Georgia and leading us to a national championship in 1980. He was a great, great quarterback for us.

At the spring game of 1982 Georgia gave me a Larry Munson Appreciation Day. Coach Dooley has his hands on Michael's shoulders. Jonathan is the little one. My wife, Martha, is on the right. My good buddy David Hayes is on the left.

Terry Hoage was one of the most gifted defensive players I have ever seen. He finished fifth in the voting for the Heisman Trophy in 1983.

To Larry
Thanks for making
Saturdays so exciting

At a Nashville reunion with (left to right) Judd Collins, who did local TV and some color on our Vanderbilt broadcasts, and Fred Russell and John Bibb, two great newspapermen.

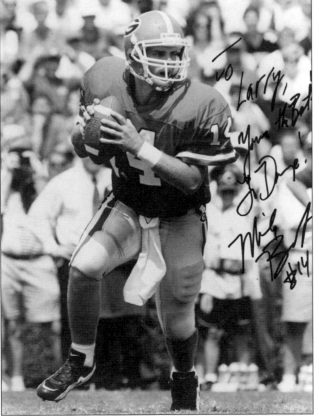

Mike Bobo was a very good quarterback for us and led us to a big win over Florida in 1997. Today he is our offensive coordinator.

My friend Dick Payne (in center with me) showed up to speak when I was honored by the Georgia State Legislature for my 50th year in broadcasting on January 28, 1997. On the right is Lt. Governor Pierre Howard. On the left is Georgia state senator Paul Broun, who represents Athens.

When I retired from WSB in 1997 the station gave me and my sons Michael and Jonathan a fishing trip to Alaska. Yes, it was cold. Michael is in the boat. Jonathan is taking the picture.

In 1999 they had a Munson Roast to benefit the Loran Smith Leukemia Research Fund. From left to right: Frank Ros (one of our 1980 captains), Wes Durham (the radio voice of Georgia Tech), me, Brad Nessler (ESPN), Loran, and Jeff Van Note (who worked with me when I called the Falcons). PHOTO

I shake hands with Lindsay Scott at the roast in 1999. Buck Belue, who threw the famous pass to Lindsay in 1980, is right behind us. That was a fun night.

This was the last Christmas party we had with our movie club in 2007. We got all dressed up and went to the Ritz-Carlton at Lake Oconee. What a great-looking group of kids. The other guy in the middle with me is the manager of the Beechwood Theatre.

I still love to fish. Charlie Whittemore and I try to get out on the lake whenever we can.

Damon Evans, the Georgia athletics director, grabs my hand at the ceremony at the Georgia Tech game on November 29, 2008. To my right is my son Michael, his wife Susan, and my son Jonathan. My granddaughter, Madeline, is looking the other way.

When they honored me at the Georgia Tech game, sometimes I smiled and sometimes I was fighting back the tears. It was a tough day. PHOTO COURTESY OF THE UNIVERSITY OF GEORGIA

Georgia, but we hadn't won one since 1982. I didn't know how much longer I was going to do this, and I didn't know if I would ever get one more shot.

GEORGIA BASKETBALL

I had done basketball at Vanderbilt for 18 or 19 years but had never gotten heavy into the basketball thing at Georgia. Then the chance came in 1986, and I did it for a while, from 1986 to 1995.

There are some pretty good basketball memories from Georgia.

I remember the coach, Hugh Durham. I remember going into his office and him saying, "We think you can help us." By then Durham had taken us to the Final Four, and I know he was still trying to promote the sport, and maybe I could help. Durham was a promoter-type guy, and he was a helluva coach. I saw him at times when he was short on talent. He would put his team in a zone and just outcoach the other guy.

We took the team out to Japan one time in December 1987. Now that was a helluva deal.

Then we left Japan and spent Christmas Eve and Christmas Day in Hawaii playing in the Chaminade Classic. I will never forget that Christmas Eve. I was sitting out on the grass in front of the Sheraton dining room with Alec Kessler. We were both moaning and fussing. Kessler had a girlfriend back home, and he said, "Man, what a great place to spend Christmas." So Kessler just gave it up and decided to go to bed.

I went inside and noticed that there were a bunch of Florida guys sitting around the bar. Florida was supposed to play UCLA in football the next day in the Aloha Bowl. So I took my big mouth and went up the bar and wished those guys good luck. I said something stupid like, "We'll be pulling for you." I thought that was what you were supposed to do for another school in the SEC. Well, that was a rude awakening. Those guys called me every filthy thing you could think of. They didn't want to have anything to do with me. I didn't realize that the rivalry ran that deep. They sure as hell didn't want any good-luck wishes from me. That made me pretty mad.

I can remember on that same trip that Durham's wife, Malinda, was just killing herself trying to put together Christmas bags for everybody on the trip. Durham was helping her. They had trimmed a tree and everything.

Between Vanderbilt and Georgia I did a lot of SEC basketball. We always had some of the most colorful coaches in the world in the SEC. Dale Brown of LSU was quite a character. Sometimes he'd coach basketball and then talk about climbing Mount Kilimanjaro to see if Noah's Ark was up there. He always seemed to be living his life for some great historical discovery. Ray Mears of Tennessee was a showman. Babe McCarthy of Mississippi State was a showman too, who really knew how to use ball control. There were a lot of characters in the SEC.

I remember that in 1966 I was out in Houston doing something for the Braves when UTEP—Texas Western—played Kentucky for the NCAA championship. Because I had called so many great Vanderbilt games against Kentucky and Adolph Rupp, I was very interested in the game. I don't know how, but I ended up in a bar with Guy Lewis, the Houston basketball coach, watching the game. During the game Lewis kept making anti remarks against our conference and our rules about recruiting. It reached me because I was an SEC guy. I was green as grass back then, but I resented it a little. But I kept my mouth shut.

I remember that we all fainted dead away when Vince Dooley got on a plane and flew to Tulsa and interviewed Tubby Smith and just took him. We really didn't know anything about Tubby Smith. I remember people in the press didn't think that Georgia was going to take that kind of a step. Tubby was a helluva coach, and I thought we were really going to make a run with him there. But then Kentucky just up and took him away. No surprise there. That's what you can do if you're Kentucky.

I finally gave up basketball because of the travel. I was the only guy on the crew who lived in Atlanta, and we would fly these small planes back to Athens. One night we had to put the thing down in Macon because of problems. One time we got stuck in Arkansas in the ice and snow. Then I had to get in the car and drive back to Atlanta at 2:00 or 3:00 in the morning. I remember the night that highway 316 opened between Athens and Atlanta. I remember it because I think I was the first guy to ever get a speeding ticket on that road. After I got a couple I really had to watch myself out there; they were really working that road. There was nobody to talk to on the ride coming back. The whole thing just really started to wear on me, and eventually that's why I gave up basketball.

But I'll never forget sitting on that grass in Hawaii with Alec Kessler. Christmas Eve. God. Who spends Christmas Eve in Hawaii?

CHAPTER 12
Champions Again!

With David Pollack (left) and David Greene (right) we finally won another SEC championship in 2002, our first in 20 years. These were two great players and two great kids.

*I thought Auburn was going
to be one of those games
that we would look back on
and talk about all the missed
chances that we had.
But there we were, behind 21–17,
we had the football,
and we still had a shot.*

I really didn't know anything about Mark Richt when he became the head coach at Georgia in 2001. I had heard that he was a very religious man, and a lot of times that sparks some discussion. He had been at Florida State all that time that they were so good, and they had all of these incredible athletes. I knew he had played some quarterback at Miami and had worked with a couple of good ones at Florida State. (Note: Richt developed two Heisman Trophy winners, Charlie Ward and Chris Weinke, at Florida State.)

All I knew was that with Spurrier at Florida and Phillip Fulmer at Tennessee, it had been a while since we had even sniffed at a championship.

But when a new coach comes in and he hasn't been a head coach before, you really don't know. Can he recruit? Can he hire good coaches? What is he going to be like during the game? Can he handle the pressure? After all, the SEC is a helluva league. We didn't know any of that about Richt.

All I knew was that with Spurrier at Florida and Phillip Fulmer at Tennessee, it had been a while since we had even sniffed at a championship.

A lot of stuff got answered that first season, in 2001, when we played Tennessee. We went up there, and they were pretty damned good. (Note: The 2001 Tennessee team went 11–2. One of its losses was to LSU in the SEC Championship Game. The other loss was to Georgia, 26–24, on October 6.) We had the lead, and then it looked like they were going to break our hearts when they ran this screen pass and scored. (Note: Travis Stephens scored on a 62-yard screen pass with 44 seconds left to give Tennessee a 24–20 lead.)

We didn't think we had any time, but David Greene led us down the field. He was just a redshirt freshman, but he was cool. I remember that Donnan wondered if he should have played him as a true freshman the year before. He was that good. He completed a couple big passes to our huge tight end, Randy McMichael, and all of a sudden we were down there knocking on the door.

When Greene threw the touchdown to Verron Haynes I did go a little nuts. I threw out the "hobnail boot" deal when I didn't know what the hell a hobnail boot was.

When Greene threw the touchdown to Verron Haynes I did go a little nuts.

But beating Tennessee in Knoxville has always been a big deal for me, going back to the time I was at Vanderbilt. It's just so hard to win up there, even if you're just as good as they are or a little bit better.

The reason that win was so big was that whenever a new coach comes in, something has to happen to get everybody on the same page and believing in what this guy is doing. After we won up in Knoxville I think a lot of people had confidence that Coach Richt was the guy and that we were going to be okay.

That was a big win because later in the year, I believe it was when we played Auburn, he got into a clock-management deal, and we got beat. (Note: Trailing 24–17 with time running out, Georgia was on Auburn's 1-yard line. Instead of passing the ball, Richt elected to run. Jasper Sanks was stopped for no gain, and the clock ran out.) People got on him pretty good, and that's tough for a first-time head coach.

But he made up for it in 2002. We had a great team that year. Greene was our quarterback and just got better all the time. We had Musa Smith at running back and Fred Gibson catching passes. We had David Pollack on the defense. We had a great kicker in Billy Bennett. That team had everything.

We got our first hint that it might be a special year when we went up to South Carolina. It seemed no matter how good we were or how good they were, we always had a dogfight in Columbia. It's a helluva place to get in and out of. The crowd is so loud and so wild. I just don't remember going up there and having very many easy games.

This was not an easy game. But the play I'll never forget is when Pollack took the ball away from their quarterback in the end zone for a touchdown. (Note: With Georgia clinging to a 3–0 lead in the fourth quarter, Pollack stripped the ball from the arms of South Carolina quarterback Corey Jenkins. Pollack held on to the ball for a touchdown to give Georgia a 10–0 lead with 13:58 left in the game.)

Pollack's play was one of the deals that as a broadcaster, you're not quite sure you saw exactly what you thought you saw. It was a little gamble on my part, but I saw the ball go into Pollack's arms, and he cradled that thing in. I saw the official (Steve Shaw), throw up his arms, and I screamed, "Touchdown!" But I had to look at the replay several times to realize what a great play Pollack made. I don't know that I had ever seen that happen before.

Pollack's play was one of the deals that as a broadcaster, you're not quite sure you saw exactly what you thought you saw.

What people forget about that game is that South Carolina had a shot at snatching that game away from us. (Note: With Georgia leading 13–7, South Carolina drove to the Bulldogs' 2-yard line with less than 20 seconds left. On fourth down Jenkins pitched to running back Andrew Pinnock. Pinnock dropped the ball, and Georgia's Thomas Davis recovered with 12 seconds left to preserve the Georgia victory.) I found out later that Lou Holtz, South Carolina's head coach, had argued with his son Skip, the offensive coordinator, over that final call.

Then we went up to Alabama and, if I remember right, we had never won up there. The game went back and forth. I remember that Fred Gibson made this catch in the end zone and landed backward for a touchdown. But then they popped ahead of us, and it looked like we might be in trouble. (Note: Alabama's Charlie Peprah returned a David Greene interception for 35 yards and a touchdown to give the Crimson Tide a 25–24 lead with 8:24 left in the game.)

Greene took us down the field again with Musa running the ball, and we put Bennett in position to save our fannies. (Note: Billy Bennett made a 32-yard field goal with only 38 seconds left to give Georgia a 27–25 victory, the Bulldogs' first ever in Tuscaloosa.) We've had a lot of great kickers over the years, but how many games did Bennett win for us?

We lost again to Florida on a day when we couldn't do much of anything right. (Note: On November 2 Georgia was 0-for-13 on third-down conversions in losing to the Gators 20–13.) So when we went to Auburn a couple of weeks later it was for everything.

I thought Auburn was going to be one of those games that we would look back on and talk about all the missed chances that we had. But there we were, behind 21–17, we had the football, and we still had a shot.

People like to talk about the call when Greene hit Michael Johnson for the winning touchdown with about a minute left, and it is one of my favorite calls. (Note: Johnson caught a 19-yard pass from Greene with 1:25 left to give Georgia a 24–21 victory. That gave Georgia the SEC East championship and put the Bulldogs into the conference championship game against Arkansas.)

People like to talk about the call when Greene hit Michael Johnson for the winning touchdown with about a minute left, and it is one of my favorite calls.

But all during that game I kept thinking about how many times we had gone to Auburn with some kind of championship on the line. (Note: Vince Dooley's SEC championships in 1966, 1968, 1976, 1980, and 1982 were all clinched with victories at Auburn.) Auburn is such a tough place to play in mid-November with the cold north wind. If you're playing late in the afternoon the shadows look different that time of year. You know it's not going to be easy, and you know that after the game you're going to have to race like hell to get to your car because those little roads in Auburn that lead to that main road simply cannot hold the traffic.

It was a great win, and then we had to play Tech, where we won 51–7, and then we got to go play in the SEC championship game for the first time. I honestly didn't know if I would ever get a chance to call one of those things at the Georgia Dome. I was used to watching it every year on TV. But it was a great thing when we won, beating Arkansas (30–3) for our first SEC championship since 1982.

When we won the SEC championship in 1982 it was our third straight. We thought there would be some more. I never dreamed that we would have to wait 20 years to get another one.

I never dreamed that we would get back two more times. In 2003 we lost a couple of gut-wrenchers—17–10 at LSU and 16–13 to Florida in Jacksonville. But we still got back into the SEC Championship Game. We played LSU again, and they were even better. They really handled us, winning 34–13. (Note: LSU went on to beat Oklahoma in the Sugar Bowl to win the BCS national championship.)

We lived a pretty charmed life when we had Greene and Pollack. After the 2004 season they were gone, and we weren't quite sure what was going to happen. D.J. Shockley had been waiting his turn to play quarterback behind Greene. We thought he might transfer because the kid was so talented. But he didn't, and we are sure glad he stayed to play in 2005.

We lived a pretty charmed life when we had Greene and Pollack.

We lost two straight games—14–10 to Florida, where we played without an injured D.J. Shockley, and 31–30 to Auburn—but we got some help in Columbia when South Carolina beat Florida. So we got

121

back to the SEC Championship Game again, and this time D.J. just played great. LSU had lost only one game, and they were ranked No. 3. We weren't given much of a shot, but D.J. just shredded them. (Note: D.J. Shockley threw touchdown passes for 45 and 29 yards and ran for another touchdown as No. 13 Georgia shocked No. 3 LSU 34–14 to win the SEC Championship Game. Shockley was named the game's MVP.)

So Shockley left, and we wondered who was going to take his place. And along came this big, strong kid out of Texas, who had a cannon for a right arm. I had seen some film of Matthew Stafford and knew he had a chance to be good. But how long was it going to take before he was ready?

We really stumbled through a stretch that season. (Note: During the 2006 season Georgia lost four games in a five-week stretch and was 6–4 heading into a November 11 date with No. 5 Auburn.) But then we got to Auburn and just played an incredible game, winning 37–15. I can't say I saw that coming. I can't say that anybody saw that coming. But we finished strong, with three straight wins. We had found our quarterback, and things were starting to look pretty good.

After meeting with the folks from Georgia, I decided that I would only do the home games in 2007. So I wasn't in Tuscaloosa when Stafford threw that pass to beat Alabama in overtime. In fact, I didn't see it. As I said earlier, my plan was always to be in my boat for that first game when I wasn't there. But television, of course, rules the world, and the game was at night. And I wasn't there a little while later, on October 6, when we went to Knoxville and got kicked pretty good by Tennessee, 35–14.

But I was there when we played Auburn and Richt called for everybody to wear black. They called it a blackout. All I know is that the stadium was full of energy. It was as good as I've ever seen. We were really, really good that night. (Note: Wearing black jerseys for the first time ever, No. 10 Georgia defeated No. 18 Auburn 45–20.)

And I was at Tech when we beat them 31–17 to close out the season. Tennessee got in the SEC Championship Game, but we got invited to the Sugar Bowl to play Hawaii. I had planned to go to New Orleans but, again, I just couldn't do it.

All I know is that the stadium was full of energy. It was as good as I've ever seen.

But when the 2007 season ended, there was no doubt in my mind that I would be back in 2008 to do the home games again. Yeah, the voice was getting a little weaker. When I left Tech that day I had no idea that I was basically done. I never, ever thought like that.

Maybe I should have.

CHAPTER 13
My 10 Favorite Calls

Lindsay Scott takes it the distance to give us the dramatic win over Florida in 1980 and launch us to the national championship. It was a call and a moment that none of us will ever forget. The early 1980s were something special.

"We just dumped it over!
26–24!
We just stepped on their face with
a hobnail boot
and broke their nose.
We just crushed their face!"

Note from Tony Barnhart: Larry's greatest calls have been widely discussed and widely reported in various media outlets over the past 43 years. But for a couple of days in February 2009 I sat down with Larry and we watched video and listened to audio of the most famous calls of his career. Some of these calls he had had not heard or seen in over 20 years. After that we picked his 10 favorite calls, and Larry gave me his impressions of them. Some calls are very quick, just one play. Other calls, like Kentucky in 1978 or Auburn in 1982, last for an entire series and showcase Larry's ability to paint a dramatic picture with his voice. I can safely say that it was two of the most enjoyable days I have ever had.

I

OCTOBER 6, 2001, IN KNOXVILLE
GEORGIA 26, TENNESSEE 24

The setup: Tennessee had apparently won the game when Travis Stephens scored on a 62-yard screen pass to give the Volunteers a 24–20 lead with only 44 seconds left. But after a short kickoff by Tennessee, freshman quarterback David Greene quickly drove Georgia down the field. Greene's 14-yard pass to tight end Randy McMichael gave the Bulldogs a first down at the Tennessee 6-yard line with only 10 seconds left. Greene then threw to fullback Verron Haynes for the touchdown. Because of Larry's call, the term "hobnail boot" will forever be a part of the Georgia vocabulary.

The call: "Ten seconds. We're on their 6. Michael Johnson turned around and asked the bench something. And now Greene makes him line up on the right in the slot. We have three receivers. Tennessee playing what amounts to a 4-4. Fake, and there's somebody! Touchdown! My God, a Touchdown! We threw it to Haynes! We just stuffed them with five seconds left! My God almighty did you see what he did? David Greene just straightened up, and we snuck the fullback over!....We just dumped it over! 26–24! We just stepped on their face with a hobnail boot and broke their nose. We just crushed their face!"

Larry's take: The hobnail boot line has really become a thorn in the side of Tennessee fans. When you say that you crushed somebody's face that is really a pretty good insult.

"We just stepped on their face with a hobnail boot and broke their nose."

That was quite a final drive when you think about it. David Greene was just a redshirt freshman, and he just brought us down the field. McMichael! How great was he in that drive? I had no idea where the hob-nailed boot reference came from. I think I was thinking about those German army boots and how those guys would walk in unison down the street after they had conquered somebody. Maybe I was thinking about jackboots and the hob-nailed thing just came out. I didn't know what it was until the next day Furman Bisher of the *Atlanta Journal-Constitution* called me. He said that hob-nailed boots had been used forever in the lumber industry up in North Carolina, where he is from. All I know is that was an incredible drive because we were gone in that game. We were done. I never thought there would be another call like the one in Jacksonville in 1980. But over time this became my favorite.

2

November 8, 1980, in Jacksonville
Georgia 26, Florida 21

The setup: Undefeated Georgia went into the game against its hated rival ranked No. 2 in the nation. During the course of the game word came from Atlanta that Georgia Tech had tied No. 1 Notre Dame 3–3. Georgia knew that if it beat Florida, the Bulldogs would be No. 1 in the next polls. But with 1:35 remaining, the Bulldogs trailed 21–20 and had the ball on their own 7-yard line. Georgia's hopes for the SEC championship and perhaps the national championship looked bleak. But on third down quarterback Buck Belue found Lindsay Scott open over the middle. Scott caught the ball near the 25-yard line and saw a slight opening when a Florida defender slipped down. With Larry screaming, "Run, Lindsay!" Scott outran the entire Florida team down the Georgia sideline for the touchdown with 1:03 left. Georgia went on to win the game, the SEC championship, and the national championship. Given the enormity of the play, many believe this is Larry's greatest call ever.

The call: "Buck back. Third down on the 8. In trouble. Got a block behind him. Going to throw on the run. Complete to the 25, to the 30. Lindsay Scott 45, 50, 45, 40!

"Run, Lindsay!

"Twenty-five, 20, 15, 10, 5...

"Lindsay Scott! Lindsay Scott! Lindsay Scott!...

[Crowd noise for several seconds.]

"Well, I can't believe it. Ninety-two yards, and Lindsay really got in a foot race. I broke my chair. I came right through a chair. A metal steel chair with about a five-inch cushion! I broke it. The booth came apart. The stadium, well the stadium fell down. Now they do have to renovate this thing. They'll have to rebuild it now.

> *"I came right through a chair. A metal steel chair with about a five-inch cushion! I broke it."*

"This is incredible! You know this game has always been called the World's Greatest Cocktail Party. Do you know what is going to happen here tonight and up in St. Simons and Jekyll Island and all those places where all those Dawg people have got the condominiums for four days? Man, is there going to be some property destroyed tonight! 26 to 21! Dogs on top! Were we gone. I gave up. You did too. We were out of it and gone. Miracle!"

Larry's take: The thing that I am most proud of about this call is that I immediately saw the block by Nat Hudson on the Florida defender. He gave that guy just enough of a nudge to give Buck time to throw. That's something that you sometimes don't see until after the fact. What I didn't see until later was how far Nat had to go just to get a piece of that guy. I didn't realize that I had asked Lindsay to run until I heard the call later. I don't think I had ever done that before. Several things really stick out in my mind. I looked across the field, and the amazing thing was I could see Dooley trying to run down the sideline with Lindsay. I didn't know Dooley could move that fast. While Lindsay was running I was trying to jump out of my chair, but I couldn't because the table was across my thighs. Every time I tried to jump up and fell back, my chair collapsed a little more. By the time the play was over the thing had folded up like an accordion.

When Lindsay scored on this incredible, incredible play I remembered something I learned a long time ago from the great announcers: just shut up and let the crowd tell the story. So I just let the crowd noise go on for a while. There wasn't much else to do, because in all of this craziness, I looked around and my radio booth was empty. Everybody had run out into the hall to celebrate.

It just defines a lot of what Georgia football is all about. If you're lucky you get to make one call like that in a career. I've been really lucky to have had more than one.

3
November 8, 1975, in Jacksonville
Georgia 10, Florida 7

The setup: Georgia had a record of 6–2 and was given virtually no shot against No. 11–ranked, 7–1 Florida, whose offense led the SEC and was No. 3 in the nation, averaging 433.5 yards per game. Florida got an early touchdown off a Georgia fumble. But the Bulldogs'

Junkyard Dawg defense of Erk Russell kept the game close by holding the Gators scoreless the rest of the way, stopping Florida six times inside the Georgia 40-yard line. With 3:24 left, Georgia trailed 7–3 and had the ball on its own 20-yard line. During the game tight end Richard Appleby had run the ball twice on the "end-around" play. This time, however, Georgia would do something different. Quarterback Matt Robinson handed the ball to Appleby, who began running to his right. Suddenly Appleby stopped, planted his left foot, and threw the ball deep. Wide receiver Gene Washington, a sprinter who would attempt to qualify for the 1976 Olympic team, was wide open behind the Florida secondary and took the pass 80 yards for the touchdown. Larry's legendary call of the play was rebroadcast throughout the state for an entire week.

The call: "4-3 defense. Matt Robinson fakes. End-around to Appleby. Appleby's going to throw a bomb! He's got a man open down on the far side! Complete! A long touchdown! A touchdown!…

"Appleby to Washington! 80 Yards! Appleby, the end-around! Just stopped, planted his feet, and threw it! And Washington caught it, thinking of Montreal and the Olympics, and ran out of his shoes right down the middle 80 yards! Gator Bowl rocking, stunned, the girders are bending now! Look at the score!"

Larry's take: What I will never forget is that I was tipped off that the trick play was coming. On Saturday morning I would always meet with Erk and offensive coordinator Bill Pace. I had done a Tennessee High

"And Washington caught it, thinking of Montreal and the Olympics, and ran out of his shoes right down the middle 80 yards!"

School Game of the Week on television the night before, so it took me a long time to get down to Jacksonville. But I met with Erk and Pace in the restaurant at the hotel. We just sat there smoking. Erk and I had our cigars, and Pace had his cigarettes. Then Erk said he had something to show me. We had run the end-around to Appleby during the year, but for this game they had put in a play where Appleby would throw the ball. Erk said, "We don't think they [Florida] remember that we recruited Appleby as a quarterback." And God, they waited all day to run it! But when it got late, and Appleby ran the ball, I knew it was coming. That was such a huge moment for us to win that game like that. I didn't realize how big it was until many years later. And when I look back, I can't help but think that somebody could have tripped or stumbled in another direction. But they didn't.

4

September 6, 1980, in Knoxville
Georgia 16, Tennessee 15

The setup: Georgia had been 6–5 in 1979, so when the Bulldogs arrived at Tennessee to open the 1980 season, there was no reason to think that this was going to be a special team. But everything changed when Georgia fell behind 15–0 and the decision was made to insert freshman running back Herschel Walker into the game. Larry's call of Walker's first touchdown run electrified the Bulldog Nation and set the stage for the most successful period in Georgia football history. Walker ran 16 yards for the score and in the process ran over Tennessee safety Bill Bates, a future member of the Dallas Cowboys. Walker scored two touchdowns on that hot night in Knoxville, and Georgia rallied to beat Tennessee. Walker's performance set the stage for a remarkable season as the Bulldogs went 12–0 and won the 1980 national championship. It also marked the beginning of Walker's record-setting college football career. In three years with Walker in the lineup, Georgia went 33–3 with three SEC championships. Walker would win the 1982 Heisman Trophy. But no one, including

Larry, will forget his call of Walker's first touchdown as a Georgia Bulldog.

The call: "Georgia knocking on the door. They are on the Tennessee 16. Tennessee has dominated this one. They gave us a break. We couldn't use it. Then we gave them a couple. 15–2, Tennessee leading. Crowd roaring against Georgia trying to make them drop it so they can't hear! We hand it off to Herschel, there's a hole! Five…10…12…. He's running all over people! Oh, you Herschel Walker!…. My God Almighty he ran right through two men! Herschel ran right over two men! They had him dead away inside the 9! Herschel Walker went 16 yards! He drove right over orange shirts just driving and running with those big thighs. My God, a freshman! 15–8! You think this isn't big, right here? Do you realize what has happened in this thing tonight?"

"He drove right over orange shirts just driving and running with those big thighs. My God, a freshman!"

Larry's take: Before the game I had people insisting that Herschel was our fourth-string tailback. He really hadn't done anything remarkable in practice, I was told. He hadn't been in the game very much when he made that incredible run over Bates, who was a really good football player. We had no way of knowing that Herschel was going to come up so large in that setting. But Herschel had a knack about him. The bigger the game, the better he liked it and the better he seemed to perform. That was such a huge, huge moment. After the game we started talking among ourselves about how good this guy could be. We certainly didn't know it after that one night, but I did know this: if Herschel Walker was as good as we thought he was, we had the team and the schedule to be pretty damn good. It wasn't long before we realized he was that good. But it all started that night when Herschel ran over Bates. The Tennessee people still hate to see that play.

5
November 13, 1982, in Auburn
Georgia 19, Auburn 14

The setup: In 1982 at Auburn, Georgia was undefeated with a 9–0 record and clinging to a five-point lead. The Bulldogs needed to keep the Tigers out of the end zone to win the SEC championship and keep their dreams alive for the national championship. Auburn drove down the field inside the Georgia 20-yard line and threatened to score. Several times during the drive Larry implored the Georgia defense to "Hunker down, you guys!" With 42 seconds left Georgia finally stopped Auburn on fourth down to preserve the victory. As the final seconds of the game ticked off the clock, Larry screamed, "Look at the Sugar falling out of the sky! Look at the Sugar falling out of the sky!" That signified that Georgia had won its third straight SEC championship and was going back to the Sugar Bowl. Georgia went on to play Penn State for the national championship, losing 27–23.

The call: "4:17. Auburn just content to complete the long drive and use up the clock so Georgia won't have enough time to save themselves…. Third down, big play! Third down, big play! Campbell going to pitch to Lionel [James]. He got a block! And he got a first down I think on the 14!…. A championship hanging with 3:07!…. First down by four and a half inches!…. Auburn is 14 yards away from upsetting the Dogs and knocking us out of everything!…

"2:55 to go! Georgia leading 19–14! Needing a play of some kind! A break of some kind!…

[Auburn is called for a motion penalty.]

"Hunker down, you guys!" "First-and-15 back at the 19. Hunker down, you guys!…. They are in a 6-4, and they pitch to Bo Jackson. One man knocks him off balance, and [Tony] Flack came up and got him! [Dale] Carver spun him three

to four yards behind the line, he stumbled off, and little Flack came up and hit him.

"Ball back on the 21, and it's second down now and 17...with 2:05 to go. Auburn trying to break our hearts here. 19–14, and the Dawgs lead. Again, you guys, hunker down!

"Randy Campbell...with a man blitzing...Carver got him from behind!

"Now it's third down and long yardage! Oh man! Two big plays! 84 seconds!.... I hate to keep saying it, but hunker down!.... Now a minute and four seconds! 64 seconds to everything!

[After a timeout with 42 seconds left, Auburn faced a long fourth-down play at the Georgia 21-yard line.]

"Ball on the 21, they have to go to the 4 for a first down. Fourth and 17. I know I'm asking a lot you guys, but hunker it down one more time!.... And Campbell, as they blitz on him, he threw a high, wobbly pass, they fight in the end zone, and the Dogs...they broke it up! They broke it up! They broke it up!

[Georgia gets the ball, and quarterback John Lastinger runs out the clock to preserve the victory.]

"Lastinger falls back on the 16 and takes a two-yard loss as they curl over the ball. Georgia students and fans standing and roaring...23...22...21...clock running...running.... Oh, look at the Sugar falling out of the sky! Look at the Sugar falling out of the sky!

"Here comes a Georgia fan running out across the field in his red pants! And breaks over towards the Dogs' bench. And now everybody...roaring...3...2...1...and they're carrying Vince Dooley off the field!

"The Dogs have won it! Somebody threw something on us! 19–14...the defense hunkered, didn't they? They did hunker! We saved ourselves! We saved ourselves! There won't be many of us in

Opelika tonight, but I'll tell you one thing, we're going to do something to Opelika!"

Larry's take: I don't exactly know why I begged our defense to hunker down, but after the first time I did it, it worked. After that I was afraid not to say it again. So I just kept doing it until we stopped them. I have no idea where "Look at the sugar falling out of the sky" came from.

"The Dogs have won it! Somebody threw something on us!"

Right after the game ended I was talking, and all of a sudden a guy in the next booth had a glass of bourbon and Coke and just threw it on us. You can actually hear me say it on the replay that somebody threw something on us. He got Dick Payne and the boards more than he got me. I thought Louis Phillips was going to chase after the guy and kill him. But that was just a great, great win for us.

6

OCTOBER 28, 1978, IN LEXINGTON
GEORGIA 17, KENTUCKY 16

The setup: Georgia's Wonder Dogs of 1978 had a knack for winning close games, and none was closer than the Bulldogs' one-point victory over Kentucky at Commonwealth Stadium. Georgia trailed 16–0 in the middle of the third quarter before beginning its comeback. Still trailing 16–14, Georgia took possession with about four minutes left. The Bulldogs drove the length of the field to set up a 29-yard field-goal attempt by Rex Robinson with only eight seconds left. When Robinson's kick sailed through the uprights with only three seconds showing on the clock, Larry did not say it was good. He simply screamed, "Yeah! Yeah! Yeah! Yeah!"

The call: "2:47, 2:46…the Dawgs desperately, desperately trying to save themselves up in Lexington…[Jeff] Pyburn going to go to

[Willie] McClendon at left tackle…five…10!…12 yards, McClendon up to the 42…2:28…2:27…2:26…. The clock just will not stop!

"Pyburn throwing to [Lindsay] Scott complete over the left side to the 35…. They hit him about the 31…. Did he get out of bounds? I don't think so…91, 90, 89 seconds…and now the clock is running against the Dawgs. 84…83…82 seconds…

"Pyburn looking at the sideline…we're on the 30…it's 16–14… 55…54…53…. The whole stadium standing up roaring against Georgia…except that little bunch on the other side…

"Trying to make them make a mistake…they go McClendon outside…he got a block! To the 25! McClendon to the 20! McClendon down to the 16! Did he get out? I don't know if he got out! 37…they called time there…

"33…32…31 seconds…. 30 seconds.

"Georgia's come flying back down to the Kentucky 16!

"25…24…Pyburn, McClendon…driving in the middle…and they knocked him down at the 12…18 seconds…17…16…15…14… Georgia calls time, I don't know…11…10, and now eight seconds, the Dawgs call time!!!! Now, guess what's coming up?

"The whole ballgame coming down to this! Rex Robinson out of Marietta, Georgia…16–14 Kentucky with eight seconds…the stadium standing! Well some of them are upside down, but they are trying to stand…

"It's going to be held just inside the 19. It's set down. He kicks it up…it looks good…watch it!…watch it!…

"Yeah! Yeah! Yeah! Yeah!

"Three seconds left! Rex Robinson put 'em ahead 17–16! The bench is unconscious! They've got to kick off! 17 to 16! Rex Robinson kicked it not *"Yeah! Yeah! Yeah! Yeah!"* quite 87 and a half yards over the crossbar towards the scoreboard! He kicked the whatchamacallit out of it!"

Larry's take: Not everybody made all the road trips back then, and so back in Athens they would have a party at somebody's house to gather around and listen to the broadcast. I found out later on that on this night they were at (Georgia athletic director) Joel Eaves' house. They were in the den, where they had a lot of pictures on the wall. When we got down to the end, everybody was trying to shush each other up and listen. Of course I hesitated a little bit after the kick before I screamed, "Yeah! Yeah! Yeah! Yeah!" Barbara Dooley told me later that the whole room exploded. They were screaming and jumping up and down, and pictures were falling off the wall.

I don't know why we were able to destroy them that way in the fourth quarter after we had dug ourselves such a deep hole. Willie McClendon had a great night. Sometimes when you look back at these old games you forget how far out of it we were and how much it took to make that comeback.

Because the game was at night, we got back to the hotel very late. My engineer just went into the kitchen and started cooking people food. It was 1:00 or 2:00 in the morning, and we had a great celebration. That was a very big win.

7

SEPTEMBER 22, 1984, IN ATHENS
GEORGIA 26, CLEMSON 23

The setup: Clemson was ranked No. 2 in the nation, and the Tigers looked like they were going to dominate Georgia by taking a 20–6 lead at halftime. But Georgia came back to take a 23–20 lead, and the score was tied 23–23 when Georgia took possession with 2:10 remaining. The Bulldogs could get no further than the Clemson 44-yard line. With only 11 seconds left in the game, coach Vince Dooley sent Kevin Butler onto the field to attempt a 60-yard field goal, which, if good, would be a school record. Again, Larry never said the field goal was good. He simply screamed, "Oh my God! Oh my God!"

The call: "The stadium rocks and swings, and the Dawgs are on Clemson's 45! And it's 23 to 23!

"64...63...62 seconds...Georgia up to the line...on the 45... trying to make something happen...second-and-9. Look at the clock saying No! No! No! 33...32 seconds...23–23. We have used up our last...time...out!

"Very big third down here, and we cannot...you know...there's just no time! But do you realize we're in this thing?

"Todd [Williams, Georgia's quarterback] running around to the right and looking...he goes for the sideline, and he threw it too high and out of bounds...incomplete...clock stops with 17 seconds...

"So we'll try and kick one a hundred thousand miles!

"We're holding it on our own 49½! Going to try to kick it 60 yards, plus a foot and a half...

"And Butler kicked a long one...a long one...

"Oh my God! Oh my God!

[Crowd noise]

"The stadium is worse than bonkers! 11 seconds! I can't believe what he did! This is ungodly!"

Larry's take: First of all, it was a helluva kick. Secondly, I will always remember that people told me they were out in the parking lots racing to their cars trying to get to their radios when they heard the roar from the stadium. They were hoping to beat the traffic, but they didn't need me to tell them that the kick was good. The stadium was just upside down. We've had a lot of great, great kickers at Georgia, but Butler was just the best when it came to making a big kick with the game on the line. Of course I was excited when he made it, but I don't think I was

> *"The stadium is worse than bonkers!"*

surprised. We knew he had the leg, and that kick would have been good from 65 yards easy. I remember later on in the bowl game we were tied with Florida State with a few seconds left and had to send Butler out there to try one that was even longer, and he damned near made that one. (Note: At the Citrus Bowl in Orlando on December 22, 1984, Butler attempted a 70-yard field goal on the last play of the game. The kick was in the middle of the uprights but was a foot short, and Georgia settled for a 17–17 tie with Florida State.)

8

November 16, 2002, at Auburn
Georgia 24, Auburn 21

The setup: Georgia had not won an SEC championship since 1982, but if the Bulldogs could win at Auburn they would earn a spot in the SEC Championship Game. At halftime it did not look good for the Bulldogs as they trailed 14–7. Auburn led 21–17 heading into the fourth quarter. Georgia made three trips into Auburn territory but could not score. But the Bulldogs got the ball back at their own 43-yard line with 3:06 left. Quarterback David Greene put Georgia in position to score with a 41-yard pass completion to Fred Gibson. Greene then threw a 19-yard pass to Michael Johnson, who out-jumped two Auburn defenders in the end zone for the score with only 1:25 left in the game. It had been 20 years since Larry had made a call that gave Georgia a championship, and he made the most of it.

The call: "We're on the 19, we've got to get to the 4 for a first down. Crowd roars at us. Man, we've had some shots, haven't we?

"Snap to David Greene…there he goes into the corner again… and we jump up…

"Touchdown! Oh God, a touchdown!

"In the corner…with 85 seconds, somebody went up high. Was it Watson or Gibson?

"Touchdown! Oh God, a touchdown!"

"Michael Johnson up high…we're gonna put glasses on it…and they stagger down into the screen and the fences…down in the corner…Michael Johnson turned around and got up in the air. We caught the ball! It's 23–21 with 85 seconds… he turned around and jumped!

"David Greene a couple of times missed some opportunities like that…

"It's 24 to 21. David Greene just threw it in the corner, and Michael Johnson, who was used a lot in this fourth quarter, got racked up in the air but hung on and had his foot down in there. We scored!"

Larry's take: What I will always remember is that the catch was on the side of the field opposite the press box and way down at the other end of the field. We had three or four guys with field glasses on it, and we just couldn't see who caught the ball right away. So I just called Watson or Gibson, and I was wrong in both cases. It was just an incredible win and another incredible play by Greene. Man, we lived a charmed life while he and Pollack were around.

9
DECEMBER 2, 1978, IN ATHENS
GEORGIA 29, GEORGIA TECH 28

The setup: Georgia fell behind 20–0 at home to the state rival. Freshman quarterback Buck Belue was inserted into the game and led the Georgia comeback. The Bulldogs finally took a 21–20 lead on a 72-yard punt return for a touchdown by Scott Woerner.

The call: "Woerner is the deep man, and now the Dawgs put seven men on the line…now only six…now only five, trying to set up a return…and Ted Peeples kicks it very well…Woerner on the 28 ran

by one…ran by another!…ran by another! 50…45…40…35…30…
Scott…Woerner! Woerner! Woerner! Woerner! Woerner! Woerner!

"Look at the stadium! Look at it!

"Now there is no sense in going away, because you know it's not going to end like this!"

The setup: Larry was right. Georgia Tech's Drew Hill took the ensuing kickoff 101 yards for a touchdown. After a successful two-point conversion, Georgia Tech led 28–21. Georgia then drove from its own 16-yard line down to the Georgia Tech 42-yard line. On fourth down Belue found

> "Now there is no sense in going away, because you know it's not going to end like this!"

Arnold behind the Georgia Tech secondary for a touchdown with only 2:24 left.

The call: "Fourth down…what a year! 2:36…Georgia, getting beat in their own ballpark…had the lead on that one beautiful run, and then Tech came back and ran it back even farther. They need two and a half yards now on fourth down. Buck Belue sprinting to the right…looking to throw…looking…in trouble…*and there's a man open!…Arnold!* Touchdown! Touchdown! Arnold wide open…15, 18 yards behind the secondary down the right side!"

The setup: Georgia could have tied the game but elected to go for the two-point conversion and the win. On the first try Georgia Tech was called for pass interference on tight end Mark Hodge. On the second try Belue pitched to Arnold, who scored the two-point conversion and gave Georgia the 29–28 victory.

The call: "They are going for two! They're going for two! [Jimmy] Womack and [Matt] Simon running backs…one receiver right…and Tech is in a 6-4 with a man out with a wide receiver…and young Buck Belue looking, and he throws. No! Interference! They knocked the receiver down! Three flags! Tech committed interference!"

The call: "Look at Tech in a 6-5 packed close! Dawgs need a yard for a possible victory. And Belue pitched the ball…*Arnold got it!* Anthony Arnold got two points! Anthony Arnold the flanker! 29 to 28! Belue faking, faking the two running backs. Started left and pitched it to Anthony Arnold the flanker, who came back by himself, naked and alone to the left…from the right side…29 to 28!"

Larry's take: I heard Dooley say this one time, and I agree with him. This game had a little of everything. They led us 20–0, and it looked like they were going to blow us out of the ballpark! Then Woerner ran back that punt, and it looked like we were in control. Then they ran it back, and it looked like they were going to take it. We couldn't move the ball, so Dooley put Buck Belue in the game. He was just a freshman; he was just a baby.

But you gotta understand that the Georgia–Georgia Tech game is a blood rivalry. You gotta understand how important that game was to us.

I just remember that Tech's Eddie Lee Ivery had a monster day against us. (Note: Ivery ran for 160 yards on 25 carries.) Man, that guy was good.

The thing people forget about that game is there was still a bunch of time left, 2:24, when we scored. They came back down the field and had a shot. But then we got an interception by David Archer to stop the drive and win the game.

But that team had been winning games like that all year. That was really something.

10

NOVEMBER 3, 1973, IN KNOXVILLE

GEORGIA 35, TENNESSEE 31

The setup: For many Georgia fans, this is the call where they finally embraced Larry Munson as their voice. Georgia trailed Tennessee

31–21 in the fourth quarter and then fought back to get within 31–28. Tennessee tried to run out the clock and faced a fourth-and-2 deep in its own territory. Fearful of giving the ball back to Georgia, Tennessee Coach Bill Battle called for a fake punt at his own 28-yard line with only 2:27 remaining. Georgia stopped the play short of the first down, giving the Bulldogs a chance to win. With just over a minute left and with the ball on the Tennessee 8-yard line, quarterback Andy Johnson tried to hand the ball to running back Glynn Harrison. The ball popped loose, hit the AstroTurf, and took one bounce into Johnson's arms, and he ran around the left end for a touchdown that gave Georgia an improbable 35–31 victory. When it was over Larry screamed, "My God! Georgia beat Tennessee in Knoxville!"

The call: "Second down. Georgia is eight and a half yards away! Tennessee didn't kick it! Went short snap! Minute 17! Minute 16! Minute 15! Second down on the 8½!

"My God! Georgia beat Tennessee in Knoxville!"

Andy going to fake it, give it to Harrison…faked it! Andy Johnson! Touchdown Andy Johnson! Touchdown Andy Johnson! What a fake! They hit Harrison dead on the 9, and Andy bootlegged to the left and scored! 34–31 Georgia over Tennessee! My God! Georgia beat Tennessee in Knoxville! Georgia has defeated Tennessee 35 to 31 in Neyland Stadium!"

Larry's take: The truth is I missed the fact that the ball had come loose. I didn't see it soon enough. I just saw Andy going into the end zone. But that was such a big comeback because that is such a tough place to play. The crowd couldn't believe the way that whole thing unfolded in front of them. The decision not to kick was not the greatest in the world. You got to have a little luck, but to our credit we found a way to get the ball into the end zone. What I will never forget is that we went straight back to the hotel because the traffic was so horrible. My engineer and I took our billfolds out of our pants and just jumped into the pool fully clothed. That was such a big, fat win when nobody expected it. I got a little wild there at the end, and later on some people told me that was the first time they had really heard me lose it a little bit. Some people have told me that is when the Georgia fans and I started to really connect. I think there is probably something to that.

CHAPTER 14

The Larry Munson
Timeline

Georgia Governor Zell Miller was very nice to me when I was honored
by the Georgia State Assembly in 1997. PHOTO COURTESY OF THE UNIVERSITY
OF GEORGIA

2008:
On September 22,
just five days before
Georgia's next home game
with Alabama,
Munson announces
his retirement.

1922:   On September 21, Larry Munson is born in Minneapolis.

1943–44: Munson serves in the army during World War II. After basic training at Fort Maxey near Paris, Texas, Munson is transferred to a medical unit at McCloskey General Hospital in Temple, Texas.

1945:   After World War II, Munson uses his $200 discharge pay to enroll in broadcast school back in Minneapolis. He graduates in a class of 20, and after a short stint at a radio station in Devils Lake, North Dakota, his first sports broadcasting job is in Cheyenne, Wyoming, where he calls University of Wyoming football.

1947:   On January 5, WKDA Radio begins broadcasting in Nashville. Larry Munson is the station's first sports director. Munson moves to Nashville where he calls minor-league baseball, hosts his own televised hunting and fishing show, and eventually becomes the voice of Vanderbilt football and basketball.

1966:   Munson is hired as a member of the original radio broadcasting team when the Milwaukee Braves move to Atlanta. During spring training Munson learns that Georgia's radio voice, Ed Thilenius, is leaving to work for the Atlanta Falcons. Munson gets the job, and Georgia wins an SEC championship in Munson's first season as the voice of the Bulldogs.

1973:   Georgia rallies to upset Tennessee 35–31 in Knoxville. At the end of the game Munson shouts, "My God! Georgia has just beaten Tennessee in Knoxville!"

1975:   Georgia upsets Florida 10–7 in Jacksonville on an 80-yard pass from tight end Richard Appleby to receiver Gene

Washington. Munson's call of "Appleby to Washington—80 yards!" is replayed over and over the following week around the state.

1977:   After living in Nashville and commuting to Athens for games, Munson moves to Atlanta to work for the Georgia Radio Newtork.

1978:   Georgia's "Wonder Dogs" of 1978 have one thrilling finish after another. When Rex Robinson kicks a field goal with only three seconds left to beat Kentucky 17–16, Munson just screams, "Yeah! Yeah! Yeah! Yeah!"

1980:   After Herschel Walker's first touchdown as a Bulldog, Munson proclaims, "My God, a freshman!" On the single biggest play in Georgia football history—the 93-yard pass from Buck Belue to Lindsay Scott to beat Florida—the words, "Lindsay Scott! Lindsay Scott! Lindsay Scott!" become part of college football lore.

1982:   As Georgia wraps a trip to the Sugar Bowl with a 19–14 win at Auburn, Munson yells, "Look at the Sugar falling out of the sky! Look at the Sugar falling out of the sky!"

1983:   Munson is honored by the Georgia General Assembly "for his great role in Georgia's championship football program."

1984:   Kevin Butler kicks a 60-yard field goal to beat Clemson 26–23 in Athens. Munson proclaims, "The stadium is worse than bonkers! Eleven seconds! I can't believe what he did!"

1987:   Munson takes on the additional task of calling Georgia men's basketball games, which he will do until 1996.

1988:   Munson becomes the voice of the Atlanta Falcons, a job he will hold for four seasons. It makes for some interesting Sundays as he travels from the Georgia game to the Falcons game.

1990:   Munson misses his first-ever Georgia game, against Clemson, because of back surgery.

1994:   Munson is inducted into the Georgia Association of Broadcasters Hall of Fame.

1997:   On January 28 Munson is honored by the Georgia State Legislature for his 50th year in broadcasting. Larry retires from his daily radio duties at WSB.

2001:   At 80 years old, Munson shows that he still has the ability to rise to the occasion. When Georgia wins at Tennessee with only five seconds left, he screams, "We just stepped on their face with a hobnail boot and broke their nose! We just crushed their face!"

2002:   On November 16 David Greene throws a touchdown pass to Michael Johnson with only 1:25 left to beat Auburn 24–21 and put Georgia into the SEC Championship Game for the first time ever. Munson screamed, "Touchdown! Oh God, a touchdown! I can't believe that. I had said about 30–40 seconds before that that you're never supposed to give up!" On December 10, thanks to a generous gift from UGA swimming coach Jack Bauerle, Georgia endows a football scholarship in the name of Larry Munson.

2003:   Munson receives the Chris Schenkel Award for career achievement in broadcasting from the College Football Hall of Fame. On April 11 Georgia dedicates the Larry Munson Trophy Room at the Butts-Mehre Heritage Hall.

2004:   On October 29 Larry is inducted into the Georgia-Florida Hall of Fame. Joining him in the new Hall of Fame class is former Georgia defensive coordinator Erk Russell.

2005:   Munson is inducted into the Georgia Sports Hall of Fame.

2006:   In a packed ballroom at the Waverly Hotel in Atlanta, Munson is honored with a charity roast. Barbara Dooley reads a letter from president George W. Bush honoring Larry's 40 seasons as the Voice of the Bulldogs.

2007:   Munson announces that he will only call Georgia's home games during the 2007 season. After working home games with Oklahoma State, South Carolina, and Western Carolina, Larry stays home as Georgia plays at Alabama on September 22. Georgia wins the game 26–23 in overtime. At the Kentucky game on November 17 Munson is named an honorary letterman and receives a letterman's plaque and jacket. After originally planning to call Georgia's Sugar Bowl appearance against Hawaii on January 1, 2008, Munson announces on December 28 that he will not be able to attend the game.

2008:   In February Munson receives the Furman Bisher Award for Sports Media Excellence from the Atlanta Sports Council. On April 4 Larry undergoes brain surgery and then goes through a serious rehabilitation at the Shepherd Center. He announces that he will again work home games during the 2008 season. Larry works the first two home games of the season, against Georgia Southern on August 30 and against Central Michigan on September 6. On September 22, just five days before Georgia's next home game with Alabama, Munson announces his retirement.

2009:   On May 4, during a banquet in Salisbury, North Carolina, Larry is inducted into the National Sportscasters and Sportswriters Hall of Fame. Larry is the first broadcaster who spent basically all of his career in college sports to be named to the Hall of Fame. He joined broadcasting greats such as Vin Scully, Curt Gowdy, and Keith Jackson in the Hall.

CHAPTER 15

Thanks, You Guys

Me with the broadcast crew. From left to right: Scott Howard, Joel Williams, Neil "Hondo" Williamson, Charles Young, Michael Williams, Loran Smith (immediately to my left), Louis Phillips, Tony Schiavone, and Mitch Ralston. PHOTO COURTESY OF THE UNIVERSITY OF GEORGIA

How do you thank all of those people? People send you stuff: T-shirts that have your words on it, pictures, and all that. And they say such incredibly nice things. I had a kid once that just came up to me and yelled, "There goes Herschel! There goes Herschel!" Hell, he wasn't even born when I said that. How does he even know that?

There are so many things that I am going to miss about being the voice of the Georgia Bulldogs. It's hard to know where to start.

What you have to understand is that nobody gets to do what I have done for so long without a lot of people helping along the way. And there were so many people who helped me and made me look better than I was.

I could have written a whole book about what the guys on the radio crew have meant to me.

There are so many things that I am going to miss about being the voice of the Georgia Bulldogs.

Dick Payne and Louis Phillips were two of my spotters, each for over 30 years. People don't understand how important a really good spotter is to the play-by-play man. It's their job to sit there with a big board and show me who made the tackle, who made the big block, and all of the things that I may have missed while calling the action. A play-by-play man leans on his spotters, and I leaned on Dick and Louis really hard.

Because the game of football has changed so much, the job of the spotter is a lot more difficult than it used to be. Now coaches substitute a lot of players on almost every play, and the spotter has to keep up with all that. If either one of those guys ever slowed down, I never noticed it. I know I slowed down as the years went on, but those guys didn't.

Payne was just incredible. He started spotting at Georgia in 1965 for Ed Thilenius, who was the play-by-play man before I got here. Early on I was paying him out of my pocket, something like $10 or $20 a game. But he wasn't doing it for the money. He just loved the work and what we were doing. When he first started out he would go to the school and pick up all the information on who we were going to play that week. On Thursday night—always on that night—he would sit down at his kitchen table and go to work on those boards.

And understand that those boards are vital (Note: A board used by a spotter has the two-deep offense on one side and the two-deep defense on the other. There is one board for each team.) He had such good handwriting. Dick did it for 40 years before he retired in 2004. More importantly, Dick became a close personal friend. He was there in 1997 when I was honored by the governor, Zell Miller, and the Georgia State Legislature.

Louis Phillips is just a brilliant, brilliant man. He was a university professor with an incredible mind. He was so quick. He is a dear friend and helped me tremendously when I was trying to come back after the brain surgery. I would have had no shot without Louis. When Payne retired I thought we would have a terrific problem in replacing him,

He is a dear friend and helped me tremendously when I was trying to come back after the brain surgery.

especially when it came to doing the boards. But Louis stepped right in, and the boards were great. Even though I didn't do the 2008 Sugar Bowl game against Hawaii, I saw the boards that Louis did where he had to phonetically spell out the names of all those Hawaiian kids. That was pretty amazing.

Neil "Hondo" Williamson came on board in 1993 to help us with our tailgate and halftime shows. Later on, when WSB took over the broadcast, he became our producer. He took over for Larry England, who I thought was an incredible talent. We were really worried when Larry left, and we thought he could never be replaced. But Hondo came in and was just great. Hondo not only did what he was supposed to, which was help Loran Smith, but he could do anything. He could read scores with a sense of urgency. He was a polished, professional announcer with a clear, crisp voice. If we needed a second spotter because we couldn't get Louis in from out of town, Hondo could do that too. Hondo really helped us when he came along.

Our pregame show grew in length over the years. It grew to three hours, and we all thought it was too long. But it wasn't because of the interest in college football and because of all the scores coming in. Loran was the perfect person to do it because he knows everybody in the South and almost everybody in one half of the country. When we were doing that pregame show he could spot somebody walking across an empty field and know exactly who they were. And he could get an interview right away because people knew him and trusted him. Loran was the guy who knew every tennis player, every golfer, just everybody who had anything to do with sports. If it was some old fullback from 1933, Loran knew him. All of

When we were doing that pregame show he could spot somebody walking across an empty field and know exactly who they were.

that helped. He is very good at what he does. Somebody once asked me how many times I have said, "Whaddaya got, Loran?" I don't know, but it was a bunch. It's hard to believe I won't be saying that again.

Later on Hondo went out and got us a new producer. That was Joel Williams. Joel had worked with Hondo before, and man, he could do everything. We immediately felt comfortable with Joel. Joel is the traffic cop up there. And we all know that if something fell down or if something got pulled loose or fell apart, Joel could pick up a sheet of scores and he would sound exactly like what he is, which is a very good announcer.

Our main engineer, Charles Young, was simply brilliant. I have never worked with anybody like him. He was so good and did so much. I have never seen anybody do as much during a broadcast as Charles Young. During the game there are tapes rolling, and eight million things are going on at once. Charles knew exactly what was going on at every single minute.

I was damn lucky to have a bunch of really good color guys working with me over the years.

Bob Younge was the first guy when I got to Georgia in 1966.

I was damn lucky to have a bunch of really good color guys working with me over the years.

Happy Howard, a general manager from a radio station in Eatonton, got involved for a little while in the 1970s. Happy was quite a character. I remember this first day, he had to do some interviews with Coach Dooley on one end of the field and had to race back up to the radio booth. He barely had 12 seconds to spare.

Dave O'Brien did a great job for us in the late 1980s and early 1990s and did the Clemson game for me in 1990 when I had back surgery. He's a great baseball announcer and is now on ESPN and all over the place.

Phil Schaefer did an incredible job in the time he was with me. He was doing basketball too. He was talented and an engineering-type guy who had to carry his equipment to a lot of these places. I remember seeing him in dire circumstances when he would be standing outside of a gym door in Oxford, Mississippi, broadcasting on the phone. He was a good veteran announcer with a head for figures. I remember that he would keep a running tally of stats as the game went along, and during a big drive he would come up with the crucial statistic at the crucial time. Schaefer was a real pro.

Scott Howard, whose first year as the color analyst was 1993, has always been a solid, professional announcer with a great voice. When you listen to Scott there is no doubt that he knows exactly what he is doing, and there is nothing that you can throw at him that he can't handle. As we expanded what we were doing on the broadcast, we kept throwing things at Scott. He just kept finding ways to get things done. When it came time for me to step down, he was more than ready to move into that No. 1 chair. There are so many more people who helped the broadcast. I will miss game day and all of the excitement of the broadcasts and working with all of these great, talented people. They kept me feeling younger than I was.

But the thing I will miss most of all is our Friday night dinners. Friday nights on the road we would all go out to dinner. Those dinners were great. Hondo used to pick the restaurant, and he always wanted to go to some Italian or French place; he didn't care how far away it was from the hotel. Sometimes I would change the reservation to the hotel or someplace closer because I didn't want to screw with the traffic coming back. Hondo caught on to that quick. So eventually Payne was put in charge of the restaurant on Friday night, and he and Hondo would huddle in the corner and make sure that I never knew where the dinner was going to be. Payne would protect those reservations with his life.

Sometimes I would change the reservation to the hotel or someplace closer because I didn't want to screw with the traffic coming back.

All the Friday night dinners were fun, especially the ones in Jacksonville before the Georgia-Florida game each year. When we first started out there were some budget constraints, but when WSB came on board they took very good care of us on the road. Sometimes the crew from Channel 2, Chuck Dowdle and those guys, would come along with us. We would walk into those restaurants and people would fall all over our table. Those were just great dinners. There would be some wine and a lot of laughs. Payne would sort of be the kingpin at the table and hold court with that great voice of his. We would give each other hell. Sometimes we didn't even talk football until it was late. We'd talk politics and other stuff.

I am really going to miss those guys.

There are so many other people to thank. All the folks at the University. Dan Magill, Claude Felton, Loran Smith, coach Vince Dooley. Charlie Whittemore, you know about. Jack Bauerle, the swimming coach. All those assistant coaches and all those administrators and secretaries over the years who were good to me. I wish I could name them all.

Mixon Robinson and I got pretty close. Still are. He is an orthopedic guy, but he looked out for me when I was having a bunch of my problems. I don't know if I completely thanked him for everything he did. But I'm thanking him now.

David Hayes is my fishing buddy and good friend. He was around when I was struggling with my decision to finally retire. I have always appreciated his support.

I need to thank guys like Don Kennedy. People know him better as "Officer Don" from that old kids' show he used to do. (Note: Don Kennedy hosted *The Popeye Club* on WSB-TV from 1956 to 1970.) I still have an old chair from that show. He called me in 1977 and asked me to work for the Georgia Radio Network doing sports. That was the thing that eventually made it possible for me to move to Atlanta and buy a house in Marietta. I remember being in that studio at quarter to 5:00 in the morning trying to get my stuff ready. I wanted to record by 5:15 and get out of the way for the news guys that were coming in. Kennedy was a real showman who loved jazz, and last time I heard, he was still playing that stuff. He once told me that if he could do it all over again he would be sitting at some small radio station in Iowa reading the news and sports.

Kennedy was a real showman who loved jazz, and last time I heard, he was still playing that stuff.

I have to thank all the folks at WSB. I did a bunch of things over there and got involved in some shows that were a lot of fun. When I retired from WSB in 1997 Marc Morgan gave me and my boys a fishing trip to Alaska. That was a great trip. I worked with so many great people over there. They were very good to me.

I was lucky because I came along when there were a lot of great radio guys in the SEC. Not just great broadcasters but great guys who all stayed with their schools a long, long time and became good friends.

Guys like John Ward, who was at Tennessee (from 1968 to 1999). Ward always got to the point. His voice was always clear, and as soon as you heard it, you knew that was the Tennessee voice. He could really paint the picture and make you feel like you were in the stadium.

John Forney did Alabama (from 1953 to 1997) and was a good personal friend. He was one of the guys they picked to travel with me when I was doing all those bowl games for Texaco. He was a lot of fun, and he worshipped Bear Bryant. He absolutely worshipped the Bear.

Jim Fyffe, who was at Auburn from 1981 to 2003, and I were really close. He was one of those guys who would spot you in the press box or come by your booth just to talk about family stuff. He didn't grow up an Auburn guy. He moved there and then got wrapped up heavily in Auburn. They called me a homer, but Fyffe, *he* was a homer. He died too soon. (Note: On May 15, 2003, Fyffe died of a brain aneurysm. He was only 58 years old.)

They called me a homer, but Fyffe, he was a homer.

Cawood Ledford was at Kentucky (from 1953 to 1992), and he was incredibly smooth with a great, great voice. He just sounded like a million bucks and was liked and respected by everybody. I thought he was still very much on top of his game when he retired after the 1992 basketball season. But the travel got to him just like it got to me.

Otis Boggs was at Florida (from 1939 to 1981), and he was a fine, fine guy and a really good fisherman. We used to talk fishing a lot, and he became very good friends with Payne. We would all see each other in Jacksonville. Otis not only did sports down there, he did a lot more than that.

John Ferguson, who was at LSU (from 1946 to 1987), did all those night games for LSU, and no matter where you were in the conference that day, when you started back to the hotel that night you were going to turn on the radio to hear Ferguson and that very familiar sound.

Bob Fulton was at South Carolina (from 1952 to 1994). Bob and I talked all the time. Whenever South Carolina played at our place he would come by my booth, and we would really talk. We grew up listening to the same guys, such as Ted Husing and Bill Stern. We had a lot in common.

The only guy in my group who is left is Jack Cristil, who started at Mississippi State in 1953 and is still there. Like a lot of guys, he began his career as a salesman, and then all of a sudden he was in the chair calling the games. And he's never wanted to leave.

I can understand that. Once you become part of a school it's kind of who you are. It's not just a job. You become emotionally invested in the place. That can be good. Sometimes it keeps you in a place when people say you should leave and take advantage of this or that.

Once you become part of a school it's kind of who you are. It's not just a job.

The younger broadcasters coming along are so much better and well prepared. Guys like Scott Howard and Wes Durham from Georgia Tech grew up with television and a million games being on every week. Those guys have so much information they have to handle when they go into a broadcast. I don't see how they do it.

I've heard people say that when my group of guys are gone, that's it. Nobody is ever going to stay at a school 20–30 years again. It's too much of a business. That may be right.

My boys, Michael and Jonathan, have been good to me. I know I haven't always been the easiest guy to get along with, particularly when I was going through all this stuff. But I do appreciate everything they do. They are good boys.

The movie group. Boy am I going to miss those guys. I actually started the group in Atlanta when I was working at WSB. We had a large group of people in that building, and you would be amazed how many would just drop what they were doing and go with us. Belinda Skelton, who is now the producer for Neal Boortz,

I know I haven't always been the easiest guy to get along with, particularly when I was going through all this stuff.

was part of that original group in Atlanta. We had a tall girl from Russia named Dana in that group. We would go to a Saturday morning show at 10:45. Belinda and the other girls loved that time because it gave them a chance to get their damned hair done before they went out on a date that night.

When I moved to Athens we started the new movie group with just three or four of us. We'd see a movie and then argue about it later. I would hand-pick the girls in the group, and then all of a sudden it started growing. It got to 10, and then it got to 14. Then the manager of the Beechwood Theatre got involved and was taking care of us.

Every year we would have a Christmas party out at Lake Oconee at that Ritz-Carlton Lodge. And that became a really big deal. The girls would all meet at my house, and we would ride limos out to Lake Oconee for the dinner. We had a mother hen named Summer who was in charge of the girls and who made sure they were wearing the right dress and would set up all the tables with name plates and everything. Summer wanted certain people to sit next to other people. It was highly, highly organized. We would go out there and have dinner, and when we would show up all of these incredible-looking dressed-up kids would walk through the lobby of that hotel, and folks would take notice. They would drink champagne, and the conversation would pick up and get loud and lively. It was a fun, fun time.

We had the last party back in December 2007, and it was a great one. In hindsight I probably made a mistake when I ended it. I looked up one time and had 41 girls. And they were just good kids…great, good-looking kids. And then I just walked away. A bunch of them tried to form splinter groups from within our old group. I was wrong. I didn't do that right.

What can you say about the fans at Georgia? They have been incredibly good to me.

What can you say about the fans at Georgia? They have been incredibly good to me. How do you thank all of those people? People send you stuff: T-shirts that have your words on it, pictures, and all that. And they say such incredibly nice things. I had a kid once that just came up to me and yelled, "There goes Herschel! There goes Herschel!" Hell, he wasn't even born when I said that. How does he even know that?

It's times like that when you realize that what you've done has meant something to the fans. I guess you're so busy when you're doing it that you don't take time to think about that kind of stuff. Now I have time to think about it.

Then I went through that thing at the Tech game in November of last year, and the crowd just swelled and the students just went nuts. And there I was, an old man trying to fight off the tears. It's a helluva thing, our fans.

I kinda wish I could spend a few seconds with each one of them and give them a little something. But I can't. All I can say is, "Thanks, you guys."

So I sit here at home and think about all the trips and all the planes I had to run to catch. All the hotels—some good ones and some really, really bad ones. Some I never even slept in. I just took a shower and went on to the next game or the next thing I really had to do.

All of those early mornings taping that hunting and fishing show on zero sleep when I was running on coffee and cigars. The years kind of run together now, and I lose track of all the games and all the big plays. A lot of people I meet remember those things better than I do.

But there are those moments that still always stick out. Those will never leave me. People tell me that they will never forget those moments as long as they live because of something I said. The idea that something I said on the radio is still going to be around after I'm gone is a pretty neat deal when you think about it. I just hope that's true.

I did a highlight video a few years back and said that if I had a choice, I would like to be remembered as Georgia's 12th man. Somebody else said that first, and I kind of like the way it sounded. I still feel that way.

All I know right now is that we've got to open the 2009 season at Oklahoma State.

How the world do you even get to Oklahoma State? And how do you get back? And what about our defensive line? Have you looked at our defensive line?

You just know it's going to be hot as hell out there.

The idea that something I said on the radio is still going to be around after I'm gone is a pretty neat deal when you think about.

About the Authors

Tony Barnhart and Larry Munson, 2009.

Larry Munson

L arry Munson was hired as the radio voice of the Georgia Bulldogs in 1966 and over the next 43 years became one of the most beloved broadcasters in college football history. A native of Minneapolis, Munson began his radio career right after World War II when he used his discharge pay to enroll in broadcasting school. He worked at stations in Devils Lake, North Dakota; Cheyenne, Wyoming; and Nashville, Tennessee, before landing the job as the Voice of the Bulldogs. He remained in that position until his retirement two games into the 2008 season.

Munson has received every major award in broadcasting. On May 4, 2009, he was inducted into the National Sportscasters and Sportswriters Association Hall of Fame, where he joined all the legends of broadcasting, including Keith Jackson and his lifelong friend Curt Gowdy.

He has been honored twice by the Georgia State Legislature and General Assembly. He is a member of the Georgia Association of Broadcasters Hall of Fame, the Georgia Sports Hall of Fame, and the Georgia-Florida Hall of Fame.

In 2003 he received the Chris Schenkel Award from the National Football Foundation and College Hall of Fame for his contributions to broadcasting and college football.

Larry lives in Athens, Georgia, where he still enjoys his first love, which is fishing. He has two sons, Michael and Jonathan.

Tony Barnhart

The 2009 season marks Tony Barnhart's 33rd as a college football reporter for the Internet, radio, and television. A native of Union Point, Georgia, Barnhart first met Larry Munson in 1975 when he was an undergraduate reporter for *The Red and Black*, the student newspaper at the University of Georgia.

Barnhart covered college football for the *Atlanta Journal-Constitution* for 24 years before stepping down from his full-time position in October 2008. He continues to write the popular Mr. College Football blog for ajc.com.

An author of four books on college football, Barnhart hosts his own weekly television show, *The Tony Barnhart Show*, on the CBS College Sports Network. He is in his fifth season as a regular contributor to the *College Football Today* show on CBS with Tim Brando and Spencer Tillman. His television work has been nominated for two Southern Regional Emmy Awards.

In July 2009 Barnhart received the Bert McGrane Award from the Football Writers Association of America, which signifies entry into the FWAA Hall of Fame. He was inducted during ceremonies at the College Football Hall of Fame in South Bend, Indiana.

The 1999 Georgia Sports Writer of the Year, Barnhart lives in Atlanta with his wife, Maria. Their daughter, Sara Barnhart Fletcher, is a second-year associate with the Atlanta law firm of Wargo & French.